Teacher Education, the University and the Schools

Using the highly successful Oxford model of teacher training and the widely respected work in teacher education of Harry Judge, a number of prominent educationists from around the world contribute chapters on a range of topics relating to the interface between the university and the schools in the complex processes involved in the initial training of teachers.

The book covers discussion of aspects of teacher education in the UK, the United States, and France, as well as in the developing country context of Pakistan. Policy issues are described by William Taylor, Tim Brighouse, and Stuart Maclure. And Jerome Bruner and David Cohen write about the processes involved in learning and thinking about what teachers need to know in their training.

This book was published as a special issue of the *Oxford Review of Education.*

David Phillips is Professor of Comparative Education and Fellow of St Edmund Hall, Oxford.

Harry Judge

Teacher Education, the University and the Schools

Papers for Harry Judge

Edited by David Phillips

Routledge
Taylor & Francis Group
LONDON AND NEW YORK

First published 2010 by Routledge
2 Park Square, Milton Park, Abingdon, Oxon, OX14 4RN

Simultaneously published in the USA and Canada
by Routledge
711 Third Avenue, New York, NY 10017

Routledge is an imprint of the Taylor & Francis Group, an informa business

First issued in paperback 2013

Typeset in Plantin by Value Chain, India

British Library Cataloguing in Publication Data
A catalogue record for this book is available from the British Library

ISBN13: 978-0-415-85356-9
ISBN13: 978-0-415-49921-7

CONTENTS

Notes on Contributors

Tim Brighouse was Chief Education Officer in Oxfordshire (1978–1988) and Birmingham (1993–2002) and Professor of Education at Keele University (1989–2003) and Chief Adviser for London Schools (2002–2007). He is currently Visiting Professor at the Institute of Education, University of London.

Jerome Bruner has been University Professor at the NYU School of Law for the last decade. His work over the years has been dedicated to understanding human cognitive processes and how they are shaped by the culture in which we live. His training in psychology was at Harvard, where he taught for two decades. He has also taught at Oxford and the New School for Social Research. A former President of the American Psychological Association, he has received honorary doctorates from Harvard, Yale, the Sorbonne, Geneva, Berlin and other universities. His most recent book is *Making stories: law, literature, life*.

David K. Cohen is John Dewey Professor of Education, and Professor of Public Policy, at the University of Michigan.

Patricia Albjerg Graham is Charles Warren Professor of the History of Education Emerita at Harvard University, where she was Dean of the Graduate School of Education from 1982 to 1991 when she became president of the Spencer Foundation, which funds research about education. She began teaching in 1955 at Deep Creek High School in southeastern Virginia. She directed a programme for beginning teachers in New York City from 1965 to 1974. The author of several books, her most recent is *Schooling America* (New York, Oxford University Press, 2005).

Professor A. H. Halsey is an emeritus professor of the University of Oxford and a fellow of Nuffield College. He is internationally distinguished, being not only a fellow of the British Academy but also an elected member of the American and European academies. He has written extensively on sociology and especially the sociology of education. He delivered the BBC Reith Lectures in 1977 and his contribution to public education was assessed by George and Teresa Smith in the *Oxford Review of Education*, 32(1), 2006.

Michel Lemosse is Professor Emeritus at the University of Nice, where he taught British Civilisation. His work for the Doctorat d'Etat was on teacher unions in England. He has published many articles on education in Britain. His *Education in England and Wales* (1992) and *Le Système éducatif anglais depuis 1944* (2000) were published by Longman and Presses Universitaires de France.

Stuart Maclure was editor of *Education* from 1954 to 1969 and of *The Times Educational Supplement* from 1969 to 1989.

Richard Pring succeeded Dr Judge as Director of the Department of Educational Studies at the University of Oxford and is presently Lead Director of the Nuffield Review of 14–19 Education and Training.

Professor Sir William Taylor CBE is currently a Visiting Professor at the University of Southampton. Between 2000 and 2007 he was Specialist Adviser on Higher Education to the House of Commons Education and Skills Committee. He previously served as Vice-Chancellor of one university and Interim Vice-Chancellor of two others. Between 1984 and 1993 he chaired the Council for the Accreditation of Teacher Education (CATE) and from 1996 to 2002 the Northern Ireland Teacher Education Committee (NITEC). At the time of the James Committee's inquiry he was Director of an Area Training Organisation and adviser on educational research to the Department for Education and Science.

INTRODUCTION

Making a difference: Harry Judge, teacher education, the university, and the schools

David Phillips
University of Oxford, UK

This special issue of the *Oxford Review of Education* is devoted to teacher education and celebrates the work of Harry Judge, whose eightieth birthday falls on 1 August 2008. The themes covered all relate in some way to his contribution throughout a long career to improvements in the education of teachers within a collaborative intellectual context involving the university and the schools and to his related writing and research.

The introductory paper by Professor A. H. Halsey sketches Harry Judge's career in the context of reflections on the University of Oxford and its colleges. Born in Wales in 1928, he attended a grammar school in Cardiff and proceeded to Oxford, where he read History at Brasenose College and later studied Theology with the intention of entering the Church. He decided, however,—and for this educationists must be thankful—to become a schoolteacher, taking a post at a prestigious London grammar school in 1954 and later gaining experience in administration as Director of Studies at Cumberland Lodge, Windsor.

In 1962 he became headmaster of Banbury Grammar School which in 1967 was to be developed under his leadership (now as Principal) into what was then the largest comprehensive school in the country, Banbury School. It was during his time in this important post that he became established as a significant national figure in education. He served on the important Public Schools Commission in the late 1960s, on the James Committee of Inquiry into Teacher Training (1971–72), and on the UGC's education sub-committee, and he chaired at various times the School Broadcasting Council and the Royal College of Nursing's Commission on Education.

In 1973 he succeeded Alec Peterson as Director of the University of Oxford Department of Educational Studies and was elected to a Fellowship of Brasenose College. He began then the process of developing teaching and research which was to transform the Department from a state of sleepy old-fashioned respectability to a position of authority and world-wide recognition for its innovative approach to

2. The early years of the *Oxford Review of Education* are described in the introduction to: David Phillips & Geoffrey Walford (Eds) *Tracing education policy. Selections from the Oxford Review of Education*, London, Routledge, 2006.
3. Ford Foundation, 1982.
4. Harry Judge, Michel Lemosse, Lynn Paine & Michael Sedlak, *The university and the teachers. France, the United States, England*, Wallingford, Triangle Books, 1994.
5. Harry Judge, *Faith-based schools and the state. Catholics in America, France and England*, Wallingford, Symposium Books, 2002.
6. Harry Judge, *A generation of schooling: English secondary schools since 1944*, Oxford, Oxford University Press, 1984.

Harry Judge and Oxford: college and university

A. H. Halsey
University of Oxford

Has Harry Judge's career reproduced in a lifetime the centuries-old history of Brasenose College and the University of Oxford? His biography and the history of his college in relation to Christian belief and modern university reform are briefly recapitulated. All tell a story of adaptation and modernisation, the man short, the college long, the university in ceaseless change from a clerical foundation through an association of colleges as finishing schools for the Establishment to a collegiate university aspiring to place itself in the 'world league' of research centres.

Introduction

Harry Judge had a contemporary, Harry Rée, who was converted to community education by his mentor at Cambridge, Henry Morris. Rée later wrote a book about Morris describing him as an *Educator Extraordinary*.[1] Judge similarly deserves that title. He entered Oxford first as an undergraduate exhibitioner at Brasenose and later returned as the University's director of educational studies after a distinguished career in school teaching, and with a fellowship in the same college. At the end of his undergraduate studies in history he intended to prepare for ordination in the Church of England and completed a second degree in theology, but found himself unable—as had so many of his predecessors—honestly to accept the dogmas that he would be required to proclaim. So he left Brasenose to become a history master in a grammar school.

How far has Harry Judge in a single lifetime echoed the history of his college, Brasenose, over five centuries? It seems apposite, as a contribution to this celebratory set of essays, to trace the history of the ancient colleges in relation to religion and to the university in order to answer the question.

The European medieval college, which began in Paris in the 12th century, was originally and essentially the invention of an age steeped in and inexplicable without religious belief and religious practice. To modernise, to escape from Christendom and to prosper in the secular post-Christian age has been the challenge faced by the Oxford colleges and, in miniature and *ad personam* by Harry Judge. So the main theme of this essay is to compare the long sweep of the College down the subsequent centuries from the 13th to the 21st century with the account given by Judge of his own 20th-century career in English secondary schools as recorded in his *A Generation of Schooling*[2] and his subsequent experience of Oxford, of Brasenose, and of retirement. We can then look at the modern relation of the University to the College in the light of the experience of a university man admitted to fellowship in his old college—an aspect of the traditional challenge to the claim of Oxford to be a collegiate university.

The Man

Harry Judge began life in Cardiff in 1928 just before Europe and America were plunged into a devastating slump as, luckily for him, the child of a lower-middle class family. His father had been born in Kidlington in Oxfordshire and had become a Welsh railway official which guaranteed a life-long occupation with a decent if modest income while other families endured the poverty of endless unemployment. Harry was a bright boy, took the 'scholarship' examination in 1939 and was offered a 'special place'[3] at Cardiff High School for Boys. His parents took the offer, conscious of his father's success as a scholarship holder at Thame Grammar School in Oxfordshire and of the opportunities for extended schooling and for jobs thereby provided in a severely hierarchical society. Harry enjoyed his grammar schooling, admired its teaching and curriculum, and saw it as an upbringing which ought to be made universal. He was a war-time pupil, a privileged learner in a provincial secondary school. He worked happily and industriously through the School Certificate and Higher School Certificate years, emerging with an exhibition to Brasenose in 1946 before being called up to the then compulsory National Service, in his case in the RAF. Trained first as a radar mechanic, he ended his service as an education sergeant before entering Brasenose to read history for three years.

The ebbing of his faith led him to abandon clerical ambition and instead to join the staff of Emanuel School—a London endowed grammar school—before serving for four years as head of the history department at Wallington County Grammar School. Teaching in and near the capital, he found time to complete a thesis for a London doctorate before moving sideways, so to say, into the directorship of studies at Cumberland Lodge[4] in Windsor Great Park, thereby widening his educational horizons and making an extended range of contacts among educationists and politicians. Then in 1968 he was offered the Headmastership of Banbury School—a grammar school which had (1967) amalgamated with other secondary schools to form a comprehensive—the headship of which he found satisfying as well as challenging. He made a success of it, was invited to take part in the James Commission on Teacher Education and Training[5] and then to become the director of educational studies to succeed Alec Peterson (of International Baccalaureate fame) at the Oxford department in Norham Gardens. Not only was that an unprecedented promotion for the head of a comprehensive school, but he was also invited to a professorial fellowship at his old college—Brasenose. He later, in 1980, took on the tutorship for admissions. In retirement he was a frequently visiting professor in several American universities and the main author of a novel and applauded comparative study, *The university and the teachers: France, the United States, England*,[6] followed by a parallel study of the place of faith-based schools in the same three countries.[7] More recently he edited a special number of the *Oxford Review of Education*[8] on Oxford and public education. Oxford and its colleges have never been far from his mind.

The Collegiate University

Turning now from the man to the institution we must first remind ourselves that Oxford has been, since Brasenose was founded in 1509, a collegiate university, perhaps *the* collegiate university despite Cambridge, which shares its medieval origins, or the American imitators like Harvard or Chicago, the 'potted ivy' league of liberal arts colleges like Wesleyan, the Claremont Colleges in California, or the 'new' English universities like York or Kent. In all these other cases the university dominates. Oxford is the last survivor of a medieval tradition and it too, in our time, is a place where the collegiate ideal has been under serious threat in the twentieth century and remains so in the twenty-first. What then is the collegiate ideal? For the present and the future it is subjected to an increasingly acknowledged threat.

The *Studium Generale* has a continuing existence in Christendom from the Middle Ages. Indeed, the European university as an institution is junior only to the Roman Catholic Church among all the public organisations of the Western world (and both, of course, have spread with imperialism to other continents, especially in Victorian and Edwardian times). The college has its origins in 12th-century Paris. Returning there in 1180 from a pilgrimage to the Holy Land it was an Englishman, Josse de Londres, who founded the *Collège de Dix Huit*, a first step in the establishment of a medieval tradition, a reply by the secular priests to the orderly progress of students in the monasteries of the Mendicant Orders, which dominated the chairs of theology, and an anticipation of what was soon to become a collegiate system in Oxford and Cambridge, where the colleges dominated the university.

One outcome of the quarrel between Henry II and Thomas à Becket was that the king declared an embargo on ecclesiastical traffic between England and Paris and decreed that all clerks abroad who held benefices from English holdings must return to English soil 'as they loved their revenues'. Scholars and masters bitterly returned and made their way to the tiny, insalubrious Thames-side town studium of Oxford to set up schools in a rapidly emerging *Studium Generale* which imitated and soon came to rival that famous centre of learning on the Parisian banks of the Seine by the end of the 12th century.

Precedence for the first collegiate foundation in Oxford is claimed by three colleges—University, Merton and Balliol. All had origins in the 13th century but even before that time Oxford had become a studium with students living in Halls. Poor students were like the Parisian '*martinets*' (house martins); they were called 'chamber deacons' (a reference partly to their menial sanitary duties). The first colleges were, oddly like All Souls or St Antony's or Nuffield, graduate institutions—that is, largely composed of fellows. In the 14th century New College began a different pattern of undergraduates closely supervised by fellows and this structure became dominant, the exception being All Souls, until it was joined in the twentieth century by a new type of graduate college.

What was the motivation for founding a college? The tradition handed down from the Middle Ages includes the ambition of the secular clergy to challenge the near monopoly over Theology of the hated Regulars or Friars. Vanity also played its part, the desire to immortalise one's name, to save one's soul through masses, prayers and candles designed to accelerate one's passage through purgatory. Charity no doubt added and perhaps occasionally took precedence over guilt money. And, more often than the cynics are inclined to suppose, there was also a genuine wish to promote some form of traditional or innovatory scholarship. Which or what combination of these motives explains Green or Linacre[9] is a difficult question and its answer in the case of previous benefactors is essentially contentious. Was Sir John de Baliol or his widow the true founder of Balliol College in 1287? What were the causes of Walter de Merton's generosity in handing over to the senior members of Merton College in the sixties and seventies of the 13th century first his manors of Maldon and Farleigh in Surrey and later his large estate near Cambridge to make the College such a wealthy landowner? What of Brasenose? Volume III of *The History of the University of Oxford* tells us that it was the combined foundation of a layman lawyer, Sir Richard Sutton and a churchman, William Smyth, the Bishop of Lincoln:

> The foundation and early history of Brasenose College epitomize the world of late medieval Oxford, and also show the potential for adaptation of a fairly conventional collegiate society. It was designed to promote the Christian faith and the welfare of church and state … . Although it too was probably intended to be chiefly a society of future priests, its clerical character was actually less emphatic than was that of Magdalen College. … Brasenose, too, had a comprehensive internal teaching system, more conventional and less grand that that at Magdalen, so that despite the familiarity of its founders with the [same circle], its undergraduate teaching more closely resembled that done in the halls. It may indeed have been taken over from the teaching of Brasenose Hall, with which its history is continuous. Both Smith and Sutton apparently had kinsmen who had been principals of Brasenose Hall in the previous century. The last principal but two was a benefactor of the new college; his successor was a fellow on the new foundation, and Matthew Smith, the last principal of Brasenose Hall, became the first principal of Brasenose College. In 1514 he was spoken of as 'Principal of the College and Hall of Brasen Nose', and Sutton's statutes referred to it under both titles. …
>
> These connections illustrate another feature of the transition from the late medieval to the collegiate university of the sixteenth century. There is no sharp line to be drawn between the 'vanishing' world of the medieval hall and the world of the Tudor university. Brasenose Hall, whose history reached back to the late thirteenth century, had already absorbed four adjacent halls in the course of time. The new foundation eventually absorbed five more. Such expansion of the site explains the rapid enlargement of accommodation in the course of the century, even if annexation did not always involve suppression. In addition to these adjacent tenements, Brasenose hired halls opposite the college in Schools Street—Black

sober and sympathetic accounts of college life earlier in the twentieth century to which Tapper and Palfreyman have added critical current footnotes. Incidentally, their plea that senior administrators be included in a modernized 'collegiality' is effectively anticipated in Harrison's chapter on Government and Administration 1914–1964, particularly his acute description of Douglas Veale who was Registrar of the University from the early 1930s till the mid 1950s. '[Veale] understood, valued and publicly defended a collegiate structure whose academic staff were in firm control. ... He loved the University and did more than any other individual during his lifetime to ensure its prosperity'.[22]

Kenneth Wheare, when Vice-Chancellor, was walking back to his college (Exeter) one Sunday after dinner and noticed a light being switched off in Veale's room in the old Clarendon Building. He waited a moment for the Registrar to emerge and greeted him with a jocular enquiry 'Writing the minutes of tomorrow's Council, I suppose?' 'Yes, Vice-Chancellor, but neither I nor you must sign them tonight.' 'Quite so, Registrar; see you tomorrow afternoon at 2.00'. They were both faithful servants of a democratic donnish dominion.

There were, John Prest has argued,[23] three stages in the evolution of Oxford: a clerical institution from the 12th century to the 16th century; an Anglican federation of colleges organised as a finishing school for the sons of the clerical and secular establishment from the 16th century to the 19th century; and finally an aspirant world university struggling to remain collegiate with rising science, graduate studies, and governmental interference in the 20th century. I don't necessarily endorse the three phase evolution—other ages and stages could be suggested—yet Prest does bring a firm historian's grasp to a complicated tale.

A more serious error is to think in terms of imperial geography. The European University is essentially an organisation of communicating persons and ideas. Originally, this meant the *lingua franca* of Latin and transport by ship and donkey. Nationalism was a long intermission. Now the telephone, fax, electronic mail, connected computers as well as the conference, severely reduce (though they do not eliminate) face to face exchanges.

So Oxford's greatness must in future depend first on self-definition: (a great confederation of colleges?; a great undergraduate teaching centre?; a great research university?; a great collection of graduate schools?); and second on its admission strategies, local or cosmopolitan. Just now it is moving rapidly towards the cosmopolitan, the graduate, and research excellence. But neither Government policy nor fund-raising capacity can be guarantors of such a future. The 18th century with its collegiate decline could come again. Who then would be the custodians of Oxford's great historical contribution to letters and science—the self-governing collegiate body of free fellows?

To give an adequate answer we must grasp the immense transformation of the 20th century which has given us Modern Oxford. Discussion and dispute is multitudinous but we would pick out for special attention a book by Joseph Soares. Contemporary history of an ancient institution it may be, but Joseph Soares' *The decline of privilege: the modernization of Oxford University*[24] is an outstanding contribution to both the sociology of universities and to the social policy of higher education. Having lived here for the past fifty years and having participated passionately in a thousand causes and intrigues round the innumerable quadrangles, committees, colleges and councils which make up the byzantine social structure of Oxford, I now read Soares as might a clan elder of the Hopi Indians gravely confronting a smart young American anthropologist. Aged insiders like me may be embarrassed by the visitor's brash mistakes (for example he repeatedly uses the American 'faculty' to refer to senior members) but we must acknowledge that he is nonetheless and essentially right in his diagnosis of our condition. He has used his 'informants' with economical skill and has analysed the records, both national and local, to present a graphic account of Oxford transformed in the second half of the 20th century. In short, from a collection of Anglican upper-class finishing schools, Oxford became a secular international university, strongly oriented to the Sciences, incorporating previously marginal women and uneasily absorbing graduate students.

Above all, Soares destroys the myth of Oxford as the greatest community of Liberal Arts Colleges inside or outside America. Instead he tells a much more interesting and convincing story of the triumph of determined academic meritocrats, remorselessly selecting the most able applicants for undergraduate places, developing the science faculties, and choosing from the international supply of graduating scientists the best research assistants for the projects of senior members. Just as the Victorians freed us from Founder's kin and established merit among Fellows, so the late Elizabethans have filled the junior common rooms and added middle common rooms with young men and women speaking many modern tongues but with little Latin and less Greek. Of course the composition of all the common rooms remains middle-class. Social equality of opportunity still eludes us. Meanwhile the internal government of Oxford shifted dramatically following the Report in 1966 of the Franks Commission. Soares' account up to 1999 already gives little space to the traditional calendar of worthies (Chancellor, Vice-Chancellor and Heads of Houses). Instead he highlights the prime movers, virtually unknown outside Oxford and even little known inside. Apart from the science barons of the big departments they were the Vice-Chairmen of the General Board from the late 1970s to the 1990s—Robert Gasser, Christopher Kirwan, Brian Smith and Dick Smethurst. These largely unsung heroes were the architects of a systematic overhaul of Oxford's internal management. They had to deal with Thatcherite cuts and, for that purpose, had to invent and apply new formulae of resource allocation. The result was that the General Board rose to equal the authority of Hebdomadal Council.[25] The underlying paradox, noticed by Soares but still shrouded in Britain by the Oxford myth, was that the State caused this modernisation. It unwittingly emancipated Oxford from the Arts and the Church of England. But in doing so the State became an over mighty master. Mrs Thatcher and Keith Joseph never intended it, though they were taken in by the false thesis of Martin Weiner and Correlli Barnett that Oxbridge had undermined Albion's entrepreneurship. Soares' demolition of that thesis is both brief and masterly. Now the question remains, can Oxford maintain its place as a 'world-class' university? Soares is convinced that future success must entail escape from financial dependence on the

State, and Oxford has better international connections and prestige to help it towards independence. Exactly what balance of state and private funding in what conditions of plurality of influence will be the subjects of sustained debate among those who guard Oxford's academic and social ideals in the 21st century.

Notes

1. Harry Rée was slightly older than Harry Judge. He went to Cambridge as an undergraduate before the war, whereas Judge went to Oxford after the war. They both started as grammar school masters and both went on to headships followed by university appointments, Rée to York to a chair of education where Eric James was the first vice-chancellor. A closer comparison of the two careers would throw light on the role of education in social mobility (upwards and downwards) in the British system. For further information about Rée see my *Democracy in crisis?* Methuen, 2007, pp. 56–57.
2. Harry Judge, *A generation of schooling. English secondary schools since 1944*, Oxford University Press, 1984.
3. The 'special place' replaced the 'free place' in 1933 as part of financial retrenchment. Free places had been intended for the very poor. The Judges had to pay ten guineas a year for Harry's attendance at a grammar school.
4. Cumberland Lodge is a conference centre in Windsor Great Park made available by King George VI and Queen Elizabeth in 1947 for the purpose of bringing together young people to discuss how they might contribute to the betterment of society.
5. Report of a Committee of Enquiry into Teacher Education and Training, HMSO, 1972, chaired by Lord James of Rusholme.
6. Harry Judge, Michel Lemosse, Lynn Paine & Michael Sedlek, *The University and the teachers: France, the United States, England*, Wallingford, Triangle Books, 1994.
7. Harry Judge, *Faith-based schools and the state: Catholics in America, France and England*, Wallingford, Symposium Books, 2001.
8. Harry Judge (Ed.), *The university and public education: the contribution of Oxford,* special issue of the *Oxford Review of Education*, 32(1), 2006.
9. Green College and Linacre College are two of the nine Oxford colleges which only admit graduate students.
10. James McConica, The rise of the undergraduate college, in: J. McConica (Ed.), *The collegiate university*, The History of the University of Oxford Volume III, Oxford, Clarendon Press, 1986, pp. 16–17.
11. James McConica, The rise of the undergraduate college, in: J. McConica (Ed.), *The collegiate university*, *The History of the University of Oxford* Volume III, Oxford, Clarendon Press, 1986, p. 654.
12. 'Regius' professorships were founded by monarchs and holders are approved by the Crown (nowadays through the Prime Minister).
13. The Readership in Education, then held by Harold Loukes, was associated with a fellowship of Jesus College.
14. Lord (Oliver) Franks, 1905–1992, Provost of Queen's College 1946–48 and of Worcester College, 1962–76; Lord (Alan) Bullock, 1914–2004, Master of St Catherine's College, 1960–80, Vice-Chancellor 1969–73; Sir John Habakkuk, 1915–2002, Principal of Jesus College, 1967–84, Vice-Chancellor 1973–77.
15. Alan Ryan, Warden of New College; Sir Brian Harrison, one-time fellow of Corpus Christi College and editor of the *Oxford Dictionary of National Biography*; Sir Keith Thomas, one-time President of Corpus Christi College. Ted Tapper is Emeritus Professor of Politics, University of Sussex; David Palfreyman is Bursar of New College, Oxford and Director of

the Oxford Centre for Higher Education Policy Studies. Joseph A. Soares is Professor of Sociology at Yale University and the author of *The decline of privilege: the modernization of Oxford University*, 1999.

16. HEFCE is the Higher Education Funding Council for England.
17. Ted Tapper & David Palfreyman, *The decline of the collegiate tradition*, London, Woburn Press, 1999, p. 170.
18. Ted Tapper & David Palfreyman, *The decline of the collegiate tradition*, London, Woburn Press, 1999, table 7.1, pp. 158–159.
19. Ted Tapper & David Palfreyman, *The decline of the collegiate tradition*, London, Woburn Press, 1999, p. 200.
20. Brian Harrison, Government and administration 1914–1964, in: B. Harrison (Ed.), *The twentieth century*, *The history of the University of Oxford* Volume VIII, Oxford, Clarendon Press, 1994.
21. J.P.D. Dunbabin, Finance since 1914, in: B. Harrison (Ed.) The twentieth century, *The history of the University of Oxford,* Volume VIII, Oxford, Clarendon Press, 1994, pp. 683–719.
22. Harrison, B. (Ed.) The twentieth century, *The history of the University of Oxford VIII*, Oxford, Clarendon Press, 1994, p. 697.
23. John Priest (Ed.), *The illustrated history of Oxford University*, Oxford, Oxford University Press, 1993, pp. v–vi.
24. Joseph Soares, *The decline of privilege: the modernization of Oxford University*, Cambridge, Stanford University Press and Cambridge University Press, 1999.
25. The Hebdomadal Council was the elected governing board of the University of Oxford until recent reforms.

Cultivating the possible: a tribute to Harry Judge

Jerome Bruner
New York University, USA

More emphasis in teaching upon 'alternatives' to the generalisation and the particulars that are being taught in school has the beneficial effect not only of broadening the learner's knowledge but of opening his or her mind to the existence of possibilities in how we know the world.

When I arrived in Oxford in the early 1970s, Harry Judge and I were already good friends. We spent a lot of time talking about our respective concerns—me on how mind should be conceived, he on how and by whom mind should be cultivated in the educational process. Pretty soon, the two topics turned into one—and they remain so in the pages that follow.

Let me say a word about those days. We were just awakening to the pervasive role of schooling as serving to maintain the social-class system, of perpetuating inequality. Education, we felt, was not just about learning, but about forming one's expectations about life. Harry had seen all of this at work in British secondary schools, and my eyes had been opened by observing the enabling effects of good 'pre-school' educational practices like 'Head Start'.

We saw very much eye-to-eye about the enabling function of education: it was not simply to 'fill the mind with knowledge' but, more deeply, to endow the learner with a sense of what his or her learning and skill made possible in the world. For my part, I had become convinced that our schools should not only transmit knowledge and skills, but should also cultivate a sense of what is made possible by acquiring knowledge, that knowledge is a launching pad, not just a stored up treasure-trove.

Harry Judge made me understand that for schools to do that, they needed to do more than just pass on knowledge, that teachers needed, each in their own way, to cultivate a sense of the possible in their students. Schools, indeed, were expressions of the culture, and in that sense teachers were central to cultural transmission.

Teacher training, accordingly, had as much to do with helping would-be teachers learn to 'transmit' the culture more effectively while at the same time transmitting subject-matter skills—granting, of course, that the latter is one aspect of the former.

How then conceive of culture, and how can we 'train' teachers to 'transmit' it most effectively? Culture's principal function, perhaps, is to *render the strange familiar.* It guides us in putting things in their accepted, 'ordinary' places. Yet, anomalously, cultures *also* provide means for *rendering the conventionally familiar strange again*—perhaps a way of readying us for surprises. No known culture is without means for doing *both* of these—the former through apprenticeship or schooling, the latter through uncertainty-provoking myth, through tale-telling (of which more presently), through the power of poetry, even through metaphor.

It is principally through the use of *both*—making the strange familiar and the familiar strange—that we (and our culture) cultivate a sense both of the ordinary and the possible. Note that we emphasise conventional rationality in rendering the strange familiar—through orderly logic-invoking discourse, through crisp 'outlining', through truth-testing and all those other order-producing techniques that we expect children to master and by which we evaluate their school progress. But it is principally through *narrative* that we typically make the familiar strange again.

What *is* this power of narrative? A story invariably begins by taking for granted some form of ordinariness in the world to which it relates. It is launched when that initial ordinariness is breached by the unexpected: what Aristotle in *The Poetics* called the *peripeteia.* The violation is then followed by an account of how the initial reigning state of ordinariness was either restored, or if not, how it got modified. To all of this is then sometimes added a *coda*, or 'moral'—an *explication de texte* like 'a stitch in time saves nine'. Stories, we say loosely, are about human or 'human-like' events or happenings and their vicissitudes. Stories do not have to be true (or false!), but they must be truth-like.

Not surprising, then, that our lives in culture are more aptly described in story form than in inflexible truth-testable logic. Stories, thus, provide just the right medium both for rendering the strange familiar and for doing just the reverse. Narrative, in some anomalous sense, is both the generator of possibility and a constraint upon it because of the requirement of verisimilitude. It provides the perfect medium for discourse in a culture.

Now back to the classroom and how we 'train' teachers. I believe it is essential to train teachers not only in their conventional 'subject', but also in the challenging arts of story telling and story generating. Let them have a logically structured sense of their subject-matter specialty, to be sure, but let them also have a more playful sense of how the world and our lives might *possibly* be. Let them, as it were, be playfully serious. That, after all, is the rich ground in which a sense of possibility develops!

Let me illustrate with an example from that grim discipline of history. It's about a lively historian presenting a lunch talk at the NYU Institute for the Humanities not long ago—the Institute being an eccentric organisation dedicated to academic fence-jumping. Our speaker that week told us that he wanted to present a 'précis' of a 'novel' he was writing, whose title was to be, simply and brazenly, *1848: America.*

He offered a succession of lightly sketched, presumably unrelated happenings in that out-of-the-blue year, 1848, beginning with the turbulent California Gold Rush, then on to how San Francisco in the ten years after grew from a sleepy little village to a thriving city of over 100,000, then on to how the invention of the telegraph at that time first changed how business firms in New York managed 'personal' visiting and then how, some years later, the transcontinental telegraph changed how people on America's two coasts kept in touch personally. Did that in turn spur the building of an American transcontinental railroad a few years further on? He ended with a casual reminder that 1848 was, as well, a tortured year of political uprisings in Europe with much internal dissent—and then sat down. No conclusions, just a string of well recounted happenings, all in that single year.

This was a 'discussion lunch', of course, and the very first questioner demanded: 'What are you trying to tell us, a 'true fable' about the origins of *modern* America, how we got to be what we are today?' 'Do I have to answer that?', our speaker replied, laughing. 'This is a *novel* not *history*! If you'd like to turn it into 'history', please feel free to do so. As an historian, I wouldn't dare!' He never budged from that stance! And just as the lunch session was ending, he inquired of us, 'What do you all think, should I publish this novel under an assumed name?' We all laughed.

That lunch gathering had an interesting 'learning' effect on me. I had never really given much thought to the doings of 1848, whether in America or in politically stormier Europe. Strolling back to my office afterwards, I found myself buzzing with conjectures. Was a new, perhaps somewhat disorderly sense of possibility awakening in the world back then? Perhaps an offshoot of the Industrial Revolution? My conjectural mood even poked up at breakfast the next morning. Perusing the newly arrived issue of the *Times Literary Supplement* at breakfast, I learned that *London* had doubled in size in the *half*-century just *before* San Francisco's population explosion. Was there something—what did I call it?—some kind of urban insouciance going on in the world at large?[1] And by dinnertime I'd even got to the point of wondering what *really* makes a 'turning point' in history.

So I began wondering why I had not been taught history that way. What way? Well, I don't quite know, except for one thing: that clever historian colleague knew a trick or two about luring us into reflecting on possibility. Ought we not, in a word, be doing more about cultivating that sort of thing in our schools?

Or better yet, should we not be encouraging a kind of multi-perspectivalism not only in our schools but also in teacher training? Some will say, of course, that such an approach is more appropriate to All Souls or the Institute for Advanced study than for Kindergarten or the Sixth Form. I doubt it!

A final word about teacher training. Remember the old saw about the fish being the last to discover water? Let not the aspiring teacher be trapped in that plight! There are many ways that teacher training can proceed in order to cultivate a sense of the possible in how one later teaches. One is by giving aspiring teachers a chance to teach in a variety of styles. I am told by dancer friends that practice in traditional jazz routines or even in bee-bop dancing makes you a better and more innovative classical ballet dancer, gives one a better sense of the possibilities inherent in the classical balletic form. Should we not be giving our aspiring teachers an early and full opportunity to try their hand at different teaching styles—no matter what they settle upon as their own 'standard' approach to teaching, if indeed they need to standardise?

I think I picked up these ideas talking to Harry Judge over our decades-long friendship. I hope he still finds them reasonable!

Note

1. See review by Paul Smith of Boyd Hilton, *A mad, bad and dangerous people: England 1783–1846* (Oxford, Clarendon Press, 2006), *Times Literary Supplement*, August 18 & 25, 2006.

The James Report revisited

William Taylor
University of Southampton, UK

The 1972 Report of the Government's Committee of Inquiry into Teacher Education and Training (James Report) suggested radical changes, many of which conflicted both with the interests of existing providers and with emerging policies on the organisation of higher education. Its proposals concerning in-service education, whilst generally welcomed, fell victim to the demographic and economic problems of the 1970s. However, the Committee's emphasis on the importance of partnership between all those involved in teacher education, and particularly the involvement of serving teachers, to which Dr Harry Judge had as a member of the Committee made important contributions, became a major theme of teacher education policy in succeeding decades.

Rationale

This paper is based on three assertions.

First, in seeking to understand the how and why of teacher education today, it helps to know something of how it was carried on in the past.[1]

In teacher education, as all else, the thoughts, decisions and actions of each generation are formed within contexts created by predecessors. At root, many of the tasks and choices faced by educators of teachers today are similar to those with which earlier theorists and practitioners contended.

Second, in the development of teacher education in the second half of the twentieth century, events in the years between 1964 and 1975 were particularly important.

Since, in common with many other activities, teacher education is today being pursued without much awareness of history, the second assertion needs to be defended.

Third, several contributions made to the work of the Government's 1970/1971 Committee of Inquiry into Teacher Education and Training (James Committee) *by Dr Harry Judge, to whom this issue of the Oxford Review of Education is dedicated, were predictive of important developments in teacher education over succeeding decades.*

Evidence to support this third assertion will be cited in the course of defending the second.

References to printed sources are listed alphabetically are at the end of the paper. Where files publicly accessible in the National Archive at Kew (the former Public Record Office) are cited, these are referenced in the text in the form NA ED xxx (file number)/xxx(section).

Background and context

The education and training of teachers in England has seldom enjoyed a good press. In the public prints it has often been ignored. During the late 1960s, however, teacher education came to attract systematic professional, public, and political attention and criticism.

Schools, teachers and training institutions were under strain, arising from both general and specific teacher shortages; pressures to expand output quickly and economically; demands from academic accrediting bodies for higher academic standards; the need to prepare teachers for new kinds of work in primary and comprehensive secondary schools, and recognition by teachers' trade unions that the quality and length of training had much to do with their members' status, salary and career prospects.

Dissatisfaction was also being expressed about the quality of teachers seeking appointment in schools, with special reference to lack of evidence of improvement as a consequence of the lengthening of the Certificate in Education course in 1960 from two years to three. The Kent Education Committee initiated a survey of the heads of its schools, and only 29 of the 218 who replied gave an unqualified 'yes' in answer to the question, 'Have you noticed any substantial improvement in the all-round quality of teachers produced by the three-year course compared with the two year course?' (Kent Education Committee, 1966). In evaluating this response it is useful, however, to remember that absence of evidence is not the same as evidence of absence.

It was also widely observed that teacher education, which had grown rapidly in the 1960s, had not been subject to any formal government-initiated review since the McNair Report of 1944. McNair had suggested such a review should be undertaken after 25 years.

The Central Advisory Council on Education's 1967 Report on primary education (the Plowden Report) called for an enquiry into teacher training. This was initially resisted by the Department of Education and Science. After rapid expansion in the 1960s and the introduction, following the Robbins report on higher education, of the B.Ed. degree, it was felt within the Department that colleges needed a period of consolidation. But, as we shall see, there were also other, less obvious, reasons why 1970 was not felt to be an appropriate time for a full-scale review.[2]

In 1968 the House of Commons Select Committee on Education and Science initiated an enquiry of its own, in the course of which it invited and considered a great deal of written and oral evidence concerning what was thought to be both good and bad about how the country prepared its teachers.

As pressure for a government enquiry grew during 1969, Edward Short, Secretary of State for Education and Science from April 1968 to June 1970, temporised. On 12 March 1970 he wrote to the Chairs of the Area Training Organisations (ATOs, the regional, university based organisations which coordinated the work of colleges and departments of education and made recommendations to Government about the professional recognition of teachers), asking a number of questions about teacher preparation.

The terms of the Secretary of State's letter did not suggest he would be content with a 'light touch' response. On the contrary. His letter referred to a 'major review' of the structure of the course, including the organisation, supervision and assessment of teaching practice, the age-specificity of training and the relevance within courses of 'the traditional main academic subject to the education of teachers of young children'. In addition, he suggested that attention be given to the 'organisation, supervision and assessment of teaching practice', the extent to which students were introduced to practical teaching problems such as classroom organisation, the teaching of reading, backward learners, and remedial education, immigrant children, and team teaching, and, in language that was to become familiar in subsequent decades:

> The content and relevance of courses in the theory of education and the possibilities of developing educational concepts in a more practical manner and deferring some theoretical aspects to in-service education.

Only minimal additional funding was offered for this exercise, but the ATOs took it very seriously. Over the following nine months working groups were set up, questionnaires issued, statistics analysed. Earnest discussions took place round committee tables and at specially convened conferences. Large quantities of facts, figures and opinions were assembled.

In the light of subsequent events the ATO enquiries might be seen as little more than a means for Ministers to rebut the idea that they had ignored critical statements such as those published by the NUT Young Teachers Association (see NA ED192/128). But from a longer-term perspective the ATO enquiry was far from being a waste of time. It stimulated staff in universities and colleges, teachers in schools, and representatives of LEAs and providing bodies to give careful consideration to what they were doing when they set about educating and training teachers. Much of this material was subsequently submitted as evidence to the James Committee. In the view of Joan Browne, the historian of the Association of Teachers in Colleges and Departments of Education (ATCDE), discussions in response to the Secretary of State's initiative helped establish a better level of mutual confidence and understanding between the interested parties (Browne, 1979, p. 207).

Alongside the ATO enquiries, several teachers' organisations joined in with their own working groups. That of the Headmasters' associations was chaired by Dr H. G. Judge, Principal of the pioneering and successful Banbury School in North Oxfordshire. The group's report, *Our Schools and the Preparation of Teachers*, was doubtful about whether the B.Ed. degree constituted the best way to give access to graduate status for college students. It also included the following passage (quoted by Hencke, 1978, p. 40):

> We are persuaded that a monotechnic institution ... cannot for very much longer expect to be regarded as a full partner with universities and polytechnics in the network of higher education.

The Heads' report was deemed of sufficient interest for a Minister to invite the Chair of the group for a discussion of its findings.

Sadly, the calling of a general election meant, in accordance with parliamentary practice, that Select Committees stood down. No report or recommendations on teacher training came from the Education and Science Committee, although evidence it had collected and considered was published (Select Committee on Education and Science, 1970).[3]

There were several ways in which an official enquiry into teacher education might have been conducted. Anthony Crosland, who had served as Secretary of State for Education from 1965 to 1967 in the Labour government, is recorded as having suggested it was possible that the Central Advisory Council on Education (CAC), responsible in the 1960s for several major reports on secondary education (*Half our Future* in 1962 [Newsom Report] and *15 to 18* in 1964 [Crowther report]), as well as the Plowden report on primary education of 1967, would have been asked to look at teacher education. It might have been the CAC's final act.

> I hadn't taken a final decision, but I think I would have reappointed [the Central Advisory committee] ... once more for a fairly quick inquiry into teacher training, and then sought a change of law enabling it be disbanded as a permanent body. (Kogan, 1971, p. 174)

But in June 1970 a Conservative Government was elected. And Mrs Margaret Thatcher, its Secretary of State for Education, had other ideas.

Origins and membership of the James Committee

During the 1970 General Election campaign, Margaret Thatcher, in her own words, had 'hammered away at seven points concerning education' (Thatcher, 1995, p. 166).[4] The need for an enquiry into teacher education was one of them. The James Committee thus represented the fulfilment of a political promise. The means to be employed for this purpose, however, were somewhat unusual.

Early in her period of office (which lasted 45 continuous months, the third longest of those of any Secretary of State for Education between 1945 and 1997 (Godwin, 2003, p. 95)), Mrs Thatcher had formed the view that the ethos of the DES was 'self righteously socialist' (Thatcher, 1995, p. 166). She also soon came to the conclusion that the relationship between her civil servants and the members of the teachers' unions was altogether too cosy. She has recorded her reaction to a Guildhall dinner held on 12 September 1970 to celebrate the centenary of the National Union of teachers:

> There were a large number of DES senior civil servants present and it was immediately clear to me that they and the NUT leaders were on the closest of terms. There were all those in-jokes, unstated allusions, and what is now called 'body language' which signify not just common courtesy but rather a common sympathy. (Thatcher, 1995, p. 166)

Given this perception, and the disenchantment of those very officials with the work of the large and representative National Advisory Committee on the Training and Supply of Teachers (NACTST), it was scarcely surprising that the size of the committee Mrs Thatcher appointed to look into how teachers were prepared had more in common with McNair and Robbins than NACTST.[5]

Besides the Chairman, Lord James of Rusholme, a former High Master of Manchester Grammar School, who by 1971 was Vice-Chancellor of York University, the Committee had only six members. The six (in alphabetical order) were Elizabeth Aggett, Head of Eveline Lowe Primary School; Cyril English, a former HMI who at the time of the enquiry was the Director General of the City and Guilds of London Institute; Harry Judge, Principal of Banbury School; Patrick Milroy, Chief Education Officer for Gloucestershire; James Porter, Principal of the Berkshire College of Education and Roger Webster, Professor of Education at the University College of North Wales, Bangor. All except Cyril English were to work on the enquiry full-time. The Committee's assessor was Arthur Luffman, a senior HMI who specialised in teacher training.

From the outset, there were worries among teacher educators about almost every aspect of the James Committee—its Chairman, who had made no secret of his doubts about the value of the link between teacher education and the universities (Elvin, 1973), its size, its remit and its procedure. However, there were hopes that the pride of place given in the first paragraph of the Committee's terms of reference to the new enquiry taking place 'in the light of the Select Committee and ATO reviews' would at least mean that the mass of information and opinion already to hand would be taken fully into account by the Committee.

The James Committee at work

Between 12 January and 14 December 1971 no fewer than 38 full meetings were held, the notes of which are publicly accessible in file NA ED 145/1 at the National Archive at Kew. At the very first meeting, the Chairman expressed a wish that the Committee adopt an informal approach to its work, with brief factual records of meetings rather than full or verbatim reports.

Impressions based on records of this kind must always be treated with caution. The Committee being small, every member was able to contribute to its discussions, but it does appear that Lord James himself, Harry Judge and James Porter were particularly influential in shaping the Committee's thinking and eventual recommendations.

In an early paragraph of the James Report, the availability of 2000 double column pages of evidence submitted to the Select Committee, plus 26 substantial reports produced by ATOs at the Secretary of State's request, is given as the prime reason why it was possible for the Committee to produce its report within a single year. However, those out of sympathy with the Committee's recommendations were quick to argue that all this prior effort appeared to have been given scant attention. Warren (1972) undertook a content analysis of the Select Committee evidence, and concluded that the James Report 'studiously avoids all but passing reference to the evidence which it had at its disposal' (Warren, 1972, p. 37).

Only a minority of members of the Committee had recent first-hand acquaintance with the institutions that trained teachers in England and Wales. Information and enlightenment was sought by a demanding schedule of visits—twenty by the first week of March 1971, another thirty in the following month. The thousands of pages of written evidence that came from almost every educational organisation with an interest in the training of teachers included much of the material generated by the ATO and Select Committee enquiries.

In a note considered by the Committee at its 12th meeting (30/31 March NA ED 145/1) the Chairman made a number of suggestions that were reflected in a paper Harry Judge prepared for the 13th meeting a week later under the title 'A tentative summary of some un-adopted recommendations'. The paper was headed with a quotation from the Department's Education Planning Paper Number 2:

> It must be stressed that this Paper is a working document intended to assist discussions of these matters and carries no implications whatever …

On the basis of discussions and visits undertaken between January and March, Judge's paper sketches a number of possible conclusions. He was writing at a time when day-to-day responsibility for almost all teacher preparation rested with single-purpose Colleges of Education or University Departments of Education. The first point in the 'tentative summary', based on suggestions James Porter had put to the Committee at its 11th meeting (23/24 March), had to do with spreading this responsibility more widely and achieving greater flexibility of qualifications. In Judge's words:

> 1. The education and training of teachers shall be the responsibility of the colleges of education, the universities, the polytechnics and other colleges of higher education, the LEAs and their schools.
>
> 2. That education and training will be organized in two clearly distinctive Cycles: in the first Cycle the emphasis will be on the liberal education of the student; in the second the emphasis will shift to professional formation.
>
> 3. The first Cycle, lasting two or three years will be followed by students in universities, polytechnics or other colleges of higher education, as well as Colleges of Education and will lead to the award either of a degree or (in the case of most students in colleges of education) of a Diploma of Higher Education.
>
> 4. A student holding a Diploma may take up employment, transfer with an appropriate credit to a Polytechnic or University willing to receive him, to study for an Honours degree, take up any appropriate course of professional training within the advanced FE sector, or enter the Second Cycle …

Judge's summary also reflected Committee discussion concerning the setting up of the Professional Centres which would be the students' base during the Second Cycle, and about the constitution and operation of *Regional Training Organisations* which might replace the existing ATOs. Groups of RTO's might validate the B.A.Ed. degree which would be awarded at the end of the Second Cycle to student teachers already in possession of the Diploma of Higher Education.

The suggested diversification of provision for educating and training teachers extended to the development of in-service work which as the 'third cycle' was subsequently to be given pride of place in the Committee's final report.[6]

Although detailed changes were made at subsequent meetings, Judge's draft found favour with the Committee as a useful summary of the direction in which it was wishing to move.

What would teacher education and training based on the 'tentative conclusions' have looked like? For the 14th meeting of the Committee held on 27/28 April, Judge circulated a document which described the post-James experiences of two imaginary teachers, 'Adam' and 'Eve'. In light-hearted fashion, borrowing the names of his fellow Committee members,[7] he sought to make a number of serious points. With Harry Judge's agreement, 'Adam and Eve' is included here as an appendix.

In June, concerned that the Committee might neglect to ensure there were enough people in the schools appropriately trained and resourced to exercise the roles that 'Second cycle' work required, Judge wrote another paper titled 'The disappearing Professional Tutor', discussed at the 26th meeting on 20/21 July 1971 (NA ED 145/1):

> Every Professional Centre (University, College or field-based) must have funds available to it to enable initiatives to be taken by it in drawing specially gifted teachers into a special relationship with itself. It should be enabled to pay fees, of adequate proportions, in order to draw practicing teachers into its work (not 'to supervise teaching practice') by e.g. attending planning sessions, contributing to discussion groups, giving lectures and demonstrations ...
>
> Should we need to say more? At the end of it, we still have not quite got a 'national system of school-based tutors'. But, as we know, some ideas can never live until they are dead.

In this, as in all his contributions to the work of the James committee, Judge's attention was focused on ways in which the initial and continuing education of teachers might best serve the improvement of teaching and learning in classrooms. When in 1973 he was appointed Director of Oxford University's Department of Educational Studies, professional tutors and an acceptance by schools of responsibility for the professional development of their own staff were key elements in the University's internship model of professional preparation, consistently praised in subsequent years by official agencies responsible for inspecting and assessing teacher education.

The Oxford Internship scheme became the best known of the school-based teacher education initiatives of the late 1970s and 1980s and a model of partnership in initial training.[8] Its success owed much to the thoroughness with which 'its approach and its elements have been so systematically and self-critically worked through' (Hirst, 1990, p. 149). This demanded lengthy periods of dialogue with, and in some cases substantial financial support from, local authorities and school management, and careful preparation of all the staff concerned. At that time the funding 'pool' to which all local authorities contributed was uncapped. This made it possible for some authorities to second a substantial number of their teachers for training as teacher-tutors, greatly facilitating the success of their school based schemes.

The emphasis in the James Report on the important role that teachers could and should play in the preparation of their future colleagues was in the 1980s and 1990s to become a prominent aspect of official policy. However, those responsible for successful partnerships in Oxford and elsewhere did not hesitate to point out that for Ministers to prescribe school-based training by decree, without additional resources and adequate preparation, was unlikely to produce better teachers and might bring the whole concept into disrepute. Experience of partnership working was to affirm the wisdom of the emphasis that Harry Judge, whilst a member of the James Committee, had placed on the training and resourcing of professional tutors.

The Report and its reception

The Committee's final report was agreed on 14 December 1971 and published on 25 January 1972. Its 133 recommendations occupy ten of the Report's 128 closely printed pages. They can be summarised as follows.

Teacher education and training should be organised in three cycles, the first to be a three-year subject-based degree course in a university or polytechnic or a two-year *Diploma of Higher Education* (an award conceived by the Committee) in a college.

The second cycle would be made up of two years of professional studies, initially in an institution and including four to six weeks teaching practice, followed by a final year as a 'licensed teacher' in a school, during which support would be provided by professional tutors in a *Professional Centre*, leading to the award of B.A. (Education) degrees to successful candidates.

The third cycle of in-service study would give every teacher an entitlement to release for the equivalent of one term in seven years and, once resources permitted, one term in five years. B.Ed degrees would, however, continue as a 'third cycle' opportunity for serving teachers.

ATOs would be abolished and replaced by Regional Councils for Colleges and Departments (RCCDEs), financed by DES direct grant, each with an academic and a professional committee, a National Council for Teacher Education and Training, would co-ordinate the work of the RCCDEs, and award B.A.Ed. and all in-service qualifications.

The proposal that the NCTET should become a degree-awarding body, additional to universities and the Council for National Academic Awards (CNAA), proved to be contentious. The debate it sparked off to some extent took attention away from what the Committee had to say about the organisation and content of teachers' education and training.

The Report was signed by the whole Committee, but James Porter and Roger Webster added a two-page 'note of extension', emphasising the role that universities and the CNAA might be able and indeed willing to play in offering academic awards of the kind discussed in the main report.

> We think it necessary ... to emphasise the very real institutional and educational advantages that could result from an association between the universities and the colleges, an association perhaps arising from the validation of the Dip.H.E. The colleges of education are certainly in no doubt of the value of their connection with the universities. We have also formed the view that this association is most likely to meet the wishes of the majority of the teaching profession. (Porter & Webster, 1972, p. 78)

Porter and Webster were also concerned that rather than ending the divisiveness of teacher training, the Committee's recommendations might actually increase it,

> ... in that area where it causes most concern: differences in the length of initial higher education received by teachers of different kinds which are in turn reflected in differences of salary and career expectations. (Porter & Webster, 1972, p. 79)

Both the Robbins and the James Committees were concerned with post-secondary provision on a large scale. The annual entry to higher education as a whole when Robbins was at work stood at some 50,000. This was reflected in the size of its own 1963 Report. Three years of evidence-taking both at home and abroad yielded a lengthy document rich in clearly set out statistics and backed by six substantial book-length appendices embodying the outcome of a great deal of systematic research.

At the time of the publication of the James Report some 40,000 students were beginning teacher education in each year. But in contrast to Robbins, the James Report appeared within a year of the Committee starting work, was one third the length, was not informed by any specially commissioned research and was singularly short of statistical analysis or projections (see Parry, 1972). Nor was there any systematic study of teacher education in other countries. The brevity of the period of enquiry—little more than ten months of meetings—no doubt played a part. The whole approach was strongly coloured by the Secretary of State's known preference for a short, sharp enquiry, with clear conclusions and recommendations.

When the Committee's report was published on 25 January 1972 a leader writer in the local authorities' journal *Education* (28 January) thought it might come to be regarded as the most important educational document since Robbins:

> ... not because of its cogency, or lack of it—but because of the strong likelihood that it will be largely applied in practice by the Secretary of State. It has the inbuilt advantage that it will not only provide a better model for the education and training of teachers but that it can offer opportunities for the expansion of higher education without having to inflate the universities or further extend degree courses in polytechnics.

These hopes were not to be fulfilled. A mere four years after the Report's publication, an editorial in the *Times Educational Supplement* concluded that little remained of its recommendations (quoted by Lynch, 1979, pp. 32–33):

> Not much is heard today of the James Report on teacher education ... [it] was first wounded by the selfish suspicions of entrenched interest groups and finally dispatched by the decline in the birth rate ...

> All that now remains of James are a few ritual remarks about the need to expand in-service and induction education regularly inserted in ministerial speeches; all, that is, except the Diploma in Higher Education.

Fairly or unfairly, the proposal for a new two-year Diploma had initially been received as a means of providing higher education on the cheap. As Porter and Webster had predicted, teachers' organisations were worried about the implications of the new structure of awards for salaries and status. Even aspects of the Report which received a general welcome, such as the importance attached by the Committee to the 'Third Cycle', were seen as likely to give rise to formidable problems of organisation.

There was also anxiety about lack of articulation and coherence between what James called the 'first cycle', that of higher education, and the 'second cycle' of pre-service professional training. Anxiety was particularly strong concerning that part of the Report which had to do with how the 'licensed teachers' whom James had proposed should work in schools as part of their second cycle training would be able to maintain contact with higher education institutions. The result, it was feared was:

> ... a very real risk of losing the coherence of content and unity of purpose which is the distinguishing feature of concurrent training. At best the cycle structure would produce continuous but related experience: at worst sequential and fragmented experiences. (Council of the University of London Institute of Education, 1972)

In the universities and colleges, the strongest opprobrium was reserved for the proposal that teacher education should develop as a 'third sector' of post-secondary education, with its own planning, co-ordinating and awarding bodies.

Lord James himself, in common with some members of the McNair Committee nearly three decades earlier and those academics and civil servants who were unhappy with Robbins's University Schools of Education proposals in 1964, appears to have had dual objectives.

First, to protect the universities from being overwhelmed by new responsibilities for training teachers, especially those who would work in primary schools.[9] The success of the University of York, of which James was then Vice-Chancellor, owed much to his policy of concentrating on a relatively limited number of subjects which reflected the University's strengths. York's success continues to this day (Shattock, 2003, p. x; see also Silver 1975, p. 13, and Simon, 1975).

Second, to protect teacher education from the academicism likely to be imposed by universities as the price of conferring degrees, not least in educational studies themselves. This problem had already shown up in the process of establishing the 'end-on', 3 plus 1, B.Ed. degree after Robbins.

All this suggested the merit of retaining a separate sector of institutions primarily concerned with the education and training of school professionals, but which could serve as Professional Centres for teachers and offer preparation for work in 'other social agencies' (Recommendation 90). There was also a sense that the College of Education tradition had valuable features worth maintaining—manageable institutional size, a close sense of community, professional commitment, a focus on teaching rather than research—which might not flourish within the embrace of universities or of polytechnics. Shattock (2003, p. x) has suggested that by failing to accept James's recommendations 'The UK missed the opportunity ... to create a liberal arts college sector within H[igher] E[ducation] ...'.

Yet from a relatively early stage in the James Committee's work, it was already clear that such ideas were inconsistent with the direction of official thinking, which favoured greater integration of teacher education with other forms of higher education.

Between 1926, when the Joint Examining Boards for the Certificate in Education were set up in co-operation with universities, and 1964, when the Robbins Committee proposed to create university-based Schools of Education as a means of planning and coordinating not only the academic and professional work of the Colleges, but also their finance and administration, the curriculum and organisation of teacher education had been increasingly in the hands of the providing institutions and within the university orbit.

When Government rejected the Robbins proposal for the future administration of the Colleges, the direction began to change. Official commitment to binary development (Godwin, 1998); the creation of an alternative route to degree status through the work of the Council for National Academic Awards, and the designation of polytechnics as higher education institutions distinct from the universities, all appeared contrary to the direction in which teachers' leaders and teacher educators had hitherto sought to advance teaching as a profession.[10]

The university link had been derided by its critics as status seeking, socially pretentious, and irrelevant—even antipathetic—to the improvement of teaching. In the eyes of its proponents it was none of these things. The status of teaching and teacher education needed to be raised not for its own sake, but as an element in a virtuous circle that included the recruitment of better quality candidates, the improvement of standards and making teaching a research based profession.

Linking teacher education to the universities was seen as a commitment to excellence. This was ambitious stuff, given the modest accomplishments of many candidates for teaching at that time. But in a society acutely aware of differences of class and status, to forge links with institutions that had higher standing was a strategy for improvement that had often been followed in the past—and would continue to be employed in the future.

Most of those active in the field, whilst welcoming a vision of teacher education as comprising three closely related stages of higher education, pre-service training and in-service development, felt that the James recommendations ignored many positive gains that the university connection had permitted. They argued that the Committee's dislike of university 'tutelage' failed to take account of the much closer control of teacher education that would be necessary if the whole 'Lord James' Tricycle' took to the road (Parry, 1972; University of London Institute of Education, 1972, p. 12).

At the 17th meeting of the James Committee on 19 May, Hugh Harding, head of Teachers Branch in the Department for Education and Science, was invited to offer some personal comments on the direction of the Committee's thinking. He said he found the proposal to set up new validating agencies for teachers' qualifications disturbing, since it seemed bound to increase the isolation of the colleges of education.

He also regretted that the Committee seemed to be so strongly against links with the universities, which were already paying more attention to the needs of the colleges than previously. In his opinion it would be 'wrong to exclude universities automatically and better to give them the opportunity to make changes of the kinds that might be recommended by the Committee'. They 'might be very receptive to the right kind of stimulus from the James Committee'. He also thought the Committee was 'optimistic' about the interchangeability of the proposed Dip.H.E between institutions.[11] (NA ED145/1)

Whilst in the Committee's final proposals the universities still had a role, the records of discussions in meetings after 19 May do not suggest the broader implications of these warnings greatly influenced the overall choice of direction or of destination.

The Government's response

It took a while for Government to produce its own response to the James Report, for reasons partly to do with changes taking place in the Department of Education's own planning procedures (see Hencke, 1978). A White Paper, *Education: a framework for expansion*, embodying the official response—and much else besides—did not appear until December 1972.[12]

The White Paper assumed growth in the school population through the 1970s, and an expansion in the size of the teaching force from 364,000 teachers in 1971 to 510,000 in 1981. However, a change towards one year post-graduate rather than three year concurrent courses of preparation, plus the effects of re-entry of already qualified teachers, would significantly reduce the need for teacher training places.

The need for some reduction in intakes had been recognised in the James Report (1972, p. 75):

> To put it bluntly, the supply of new teachers is now increasing so rapidly that it must soon catch up with any likely assessment of future demand, and choices will have to be made very soon about various ways of using or diverting some of the resources at present invested in the education and training of teachers.

The Committee did not, however, offer any detailed calculations. Records of the Committee's meetings show the main reason to have been that in 1971 the Department was not in a position to provide reliable figures.[13] Harding (1978, p. 633) later stated that the Committee had been given a paper indicating how soon and by how much the teacher training system might need to contract, but that as far as he knew 'it did not affect the Report's recommendations'. A chapter on demographics and finance had been drafted, but when it came to writing the final report, the notes for the 28th meeting, held on 28 September 1971, state that:

> The report should include a discussion in general terms of teacher supply. It would be necessary to draw attention to those proposals which called for an improved overall staffing ratio but inadvisable to quote a figure, even as an example, or to include tables of output from Cycle 2 courses.

The decision not to consider numbers in detail no doubt reflected advice from the Treasury and the Department, which does not appear to have been resisted. There was, however, an understanding that both numbers and funding would receive attention following publication of the Committee's Report. From the notes of the Committee's meetings and from the Report itself (see p. 75), it also seems too much hope rested on being able to accommodate 'Third Cycle' numbers and students enrolling for the new Dip.H.E. in college space freed up by declining numbers in initial training. In the event, the recession of the early 1970s precluded funding at the level needed to implement the Committee's ambitious 'Third Cycle' proposals.

The White Paper began the process of integrating teacher education into a diversified post-secondary system. During the remainder of the 1970s, with colleges closing or merging with universities, polytechnics and other further and higher education institutions, a whole sector of higher education was to disappear. This fundamentally changed the relationship between academic and administrative responsibilities for teacher education which McNair, Robbins and then James had sought to clarify, and made the James Committee's proposals for funding and co-coordinating the work of Colleges of Education redundant. But it was not until the establishment of the Teacher Training Agency in 1993 that the distribution of academic and administrative responsibilities was fully addressed, and in a context of higher education provision and institutional governance radically different from 1944, 1963 or 1972.

Almost alone among its major recommendations, what the James Committee had to say about in-service training met with widespread approval and official endorsement. Throughout the 1950s and 1960s many Training Colleges/Colleges of Education had already taken an active part in the continued professional development of serving teachers. This included short courses and events in many aspects of primary and secondary teaching, programmes of study leading to advanced certificates and diplomas, and in some places, part-time B.Ed courses. Where James broke new ground was in suggesting that teachers should be able to take one term's full-time release in every seven years of service. This would improve to one term in five as resources became more freely available.

Also endorsed by the 1972 White Paper, the two year Diploma of Higher Education, although not without its supporters and able to demonstrate some successes, never really achieved the hopes invested in it, being overtaken by the expansion of degree level work in the growing number of polytechnics and their subsequent re-designation as universities.

Consideration of the James recommendation that Regional Councils for Colleges and Departments (RCCTEs) should replace the Area Training Organisations was vitiated by the understandable preference of local authorities for a regional organisation that would unify, rather than further divide, all forms of non-university advanced further and higher education. No RCCTE was ever set up.

Conclusion

Although many of the reforms proposed in its Report could not be implemented in the form proposed, this does not rob the James Committee of its importance in the history of teacher education in the second half of the 20th century, nor diminish the value of particular contributions that members made to its deliberations, several of which now influence 21st- century practice.

The Committee focused attention on the organisation of teacher education and the integration of its stages. But it did so at a time when the institutional base of higher education was shifting. What could not have been foreseen was how during the 1980s and 1990s mass higher education would fundamentally alter many of the assumptions on which Committee's work had been based. Universities and polytechnics came to provide a wide spectrum of vocational courses for occupations many of which had hardly existed in the 1960s and 1970s, and the technical orientation of the polytechnic tradition was significantly weakened in the face of demand from students for opportunities to study arts and professional subjects.[14]

The Committee had neither time nor resources to consider the wider range of possibilities and constraints that were soon to become apparent. The political commitment which led to it being set up at the end of 1970, coupled with shortness of time, did not chime with the direction and more measured pace of resource-based planning in response to impending demographic and economic pressures. The eventual outcome vindicated the views of those within and beyond the Department of Education and Science who believed that 1970 was not an opportune time to consider the future of teacher education in isolation from wider issues of post-secondary provision. For once, the much derided excuse of 'unripe time' was justified.

Teachers must always have something to teach. They must know about children and schools and be trained in the skills that facilitate learning. They must have opportunities to practice the use of this knowledge and skill in real classrooms and to learn from the feedback provided by pupils, experienced teachers and their tutors. These elements should cohere in a way that enables the beginning teacher to make a sound start and to go on learning and improving throughout her or his career.

Such requirements are as central to the formation of teachers today as they were in 1972. Harry Judge, James Porter and the Chairman and other members of the James Committee sought to satisfy them in three main ways. First, by encouraging teacher education and training to be seen as a life-long rather than a short term, one-off process. Second, by a focus on teacher preparation which would give substance to the long-heard rhetoric of full involvement by schools and serving teachers in the formation of new members of the profession. Third, by proposing organisational arrangements which would introduce greater flexibility into initial preparation, closing the gaps between the stages of teachers' education, training and professional development and between university and college routes into teaching. But their proposals were formulated at a time when seismic shifts were about to take place in the demographic, economic and administrative context of education beyond 18 which would render obsolete the design of the edifice that in good faith and in accordance with their remit they sought to construct.

The integration of the 'three cycles'—higher education, initial professional training and induction, and in-service development—was central to the James Report's philosophy. If economic conditions had been more propitious during the 1970s, wide ranging and inclusive 'Third Cycle' programmes could have begun to make a difference to the quality of teaching and learning in schools that might have headed off some of the attacks on teacher education that characterised the early 1980s. As it was, implementation of a coherent 'James style' sequence of teacher formation, based on establishing strong connections between the three cycles, took a long time to arrive. It was not until the 1990s that the reform of teacher education in Northern Ireland, with mandatory induction and early professional development, and related developments in Scotland and England, put in place opportunities which today, apart from inevitable arguments about the availability of resources and the priorities that determine their distribution, appear to arouse little fundamental dissent.

The stronger and more structured contributions from serving teachers to the initial training of their future colleagues, on which Harry Judge had placed so much emphasis in his contributions to the discussions of the James Committee and in his subsequent work at Oxford, are now prominent features of the training courses offered by universities and the basis of a variety of school-based and employment routes into teaching.

The study of education, not least in our most prestigious, research intensive universities, is today perceived as 'a proper, grown-up subject' a status which it had to struggle hard to achieve in earlier decades. However, there is now very little time in which to offer during initial training even a modest introduction to the forms of thought—historical, philosophical, psychological and sociological—which underlie educational principles and practice. Furthermore, although courses for advanced qualifications in professional specialisms and for the M.Ed and D.Ed are booming, there are too few opportunities for serving teachers in this country to be seconded for significant periods of full-time study. It has also to be asked if in our now much more tightly regulated and supervised schools, there are always sufficient opportunities to apply the outcomes of advanced study and research to the improvement of practice and performance.

As school principal, an influential member of the James Committee, Director of Oxford University's Department of Educational Studies, as well as through his studies of teacher education abroad and in the other ways celebrated in this issue of the *Oxford Review of Education*, Harry Judge has consistently focused on structures and processes which improve teaching and learning in classrooms, and has made valuable contributions to how we think and act when we set out to educate. We have good reasons to be grateful to him, and to wish him well in his 80th year.

Acknowledgment

I am grateful to Dr C. D. Godwin for earlier archive work on the James Committee files in the then Public Record Office (now National Archive), undertaken in the course of research on the history of teacher education supported by an Emeritus Fellowship awarded to me by the Leverhulme Foundation.

Notes

1. At the time of the James Report there were two main ways in England in which to obtain a qualification to teach in primary schools (generally 5–11) and secondary schools (generally

11–18, but 11–16/16–18 in some areas). Most of those wanting to teach in primary schools and some who wished to work in secondary entered Colleges of Education direct from school at 18 or, in the case of the minority of 'mature students', after periods of employment, to pursue what from 1960 had become a three year (previously two year) course for a *Certificate of Education.* These courses were *concurrent,* i.e. both subject and professional studies were pursued throughout the three years. Following the Robbins Report on Higher Education of 1963, a proportion (10–25%) of College of Education students had the opportunity to add a fourth year of college-based but university validated and supervised study for a *Bachelor of Education* (B.Ed.) degree. Most teachers in sec ondary schools qualified by means of the *consecutive* route. After attaining a Bachelor's degree in an arts or science subject or subjects they undertook a year's study in a university department of education or college of education leading to the award of a *Post-graduate Certificate of Education (PGCE).* Practical work in schools (*'School practice'*) featured in both concurrent and consecutive courses. Today, there are many more ways in which to become a qualified teacher. Details of the variety of routes that exist can be obtained from the Training and Development Agency (TDA) website at: http://www.tda.gov.uk/Recruit/becomingateacher.aspx.

2. The debate within the Department concerning whether an enquiry should be held, and if so, the form it should take, is documented in NA ED192/128.
3. In the course of his meeting with the James Committee on 6 April 1971 the Chairman of the Select Committee, Fred Willey MP, said that if his Committee *had* reported, it would only have offered 'broad guidelines' (NA ED145/1). He also argued elsewhere that much of the evidence given to the Committee constituted a *prima facie* case for a 'thorough examination' of teacher training (Willey & Maddison, 1971).
4. The other six points were a greater priority for primary education; the expansion of nursery education; freedom for LEAs to decide the future of their secondary education arrangements, whilst avoiding making 'irrevocable changes to any good school unless ... the alternative is better'; raising the school leaving age to 16; encouraging direct grant schools and retaining independent schools, and expanding higher and further education (Thatcher, 1995, p. 167).
5. The McNair Committee had 11 members, Robbins 12.
6. The reasons for this are set out in the note of the 26th meeting on 20/21 July 1971: 'It was suggested that the first item in the main body of the Report might be Cycle 3, since the expansion of in service training was the one subject for which there was unanimous support in the evidence and it affected recommendations about Cycle 2'.
7. And one other.
8. For more details of the Oxford scheme see Benton (1990), which includes a chapter on the reform of initial training written by Harry Judge. Brookes (2003) has usefully summarised evidence that quality of mentoring in schools is critical to the level of success achieved by the substantial number of graduates who now qualify by means of the employment-based Graduate Teacher Programme (GTP).
9. At one rather fraught meeting between the Chairman and members of the James Committee and officers of the University Council for the Education of Teachers in July 1971, at which the involvement of the universities in the ATOs was under discussion, Lord James had spoken of 'freeing the universities to get on with their own work'. This had horrified UCET representatives, who saw that universities had a vital interest in how the teachers of their future students were educated and trained.
10. For its part, the Council for National Academic Awards had on 22 February 1972, less than a month after publication of the James Report, minuted that 'Without prejudging the final outcome of a detailed study of the proposals, it seemed to the Council at this stage that the proposal to set up a new body or bodies to administer the awards was open to serious question', and that 'Council should be prepared to validate the Dip H.E.' (Minutes of Council of the

CNAA 22 February 1972, 518, 1–3, held in the Modern Records Centre at the University of Warwick).

11. Clear indications of the way in which Harding and his colleagues in the Department had been thinking were given in a speech at a Conference of College Principals held in York in June 1970. The mimeographed Report of the Conference was not published but circulated widely in the teacher education community. (See also Harding, 1978.)
12. The text of the written statement by the Prime Minister launching the White Paper repays careful study and can be accessed at: http://www.margaretthatcher.org/speeches/displaydocument.asp?docid=102233.
13. The Committee had requested information from the Department about the number of teachers required in 1971, 1976 and 1981. It is recorded that when he met the Committee at its 17th meeting on 19th May 1971, Hugh Harding said:

    > ... no answer could be given to this question, since an estimate of the prospective size of the teacher force depended on assumptions and policies not yet settled or adopted. It was now fairly generally accepted that staffing policies could not be satisfactorily expressed in terms of the elimination of oversized classes; if a national staffing policy were adopted, it was likely that it would be expressed in terms of a target figure for the pupil/teacher ratio ... If it were decided to stabilize the staffing of the schools at a given pupil/teacher ratio, this would imply a reduction in the recruitment of new teachers and consequently in the number of training places required. An increase in the proportion of graduate recruits (who would only need one year of training instead of three) would further reduce the total size of the teacher training establishment required. (NA ED 145/1)

    In her speech in January 1971 to the annual North of England Conference (a familiar venue for airing important policy changes), Margaret Thatcher had raised for the first time in public the question of whether it would be right to continue the high level of teacher output already achieved into the second half of the 1970s. It was also the case that the Department had only recently established a new internal planning organisation.
14. In the early 1980s it was confidently assuming that we were in for a period of declining numbers in higher education, and should manage for contraction. Nicolas Nassim Taleb's two books *Fooled by Randomness* (2004) and *Black Swan* (2007) offer valuable lessons about the limitations of projections and predictions in strategic planning.

References

Association of Teachers in Colleges and Departments of Education. (1972) *A statement by the Executive Committee on Teacher Education and Training* (London, Association of Teachers).

Benton, P. (Ed.) (1990) *The Oxford Internship Scheme: integration and partnership in initial teacher education* (London, Calouste Gulbenkian Foundation).

Brookes, W. (2003) GTP training—is adequate good enough? Paper presented to the *Annual Conference of the British Educational Research Association,* Edinburgh, 11–13 September.

Browne, J. D. (1979) *Teachers of teachers: a history of the Association of Teachers in Colleges and Departments of Education* (London, Hodder).

Council of the University of London Institute of Education. (1972) *A statement by the Council of the Institute on the James Report* (London, University of London Institute of Education).

Education (1972) (The Local Education Authorities' journal) Second only to Robbins? 28 January.

Elvin, H. L. (1973) The question of teacher training, in: H. Hawton (Ed.) *Question 6* (London, Pemberton Press).

Elvin, H. L. & Peters, R. S. (1972) The James report and the University of London, paper for University of London Institute of Education Committees (mimeo).

Godwin, C. D. (1998) The origin of the binary system, *History of Education,* 27(2), 171–191.

Godwin, C. D. (2003) Policy-making without partners: the NACTST and its demise 1965–73, *History of Education,* 32(1), 81–100.

Harding, H. (1978) Harding replies to Hencke over College closures, *Education,* 29 December.

Hencke, D. (1978) *Colleges in crisis* (Harmondsworth, Penguin).

Hirst, P. J. (1990) Internship: a view from outside, in: P. Benton (Ed.) *The Oxford Internship Scheme: integration and partnership in initial teacher education* (London, Calouste Gulbenkian Foundation).

House of Commons Select Committee on Education and Science. (1969–1970) *Teacher training volume 1: full committee evidence and appendices* (London, HMSO).

James Report. (1972) *Teacher education and training: a report by a Committee of Inquiry appointed by the Secretary of State for Education and Science, under the chairmanship of Lord James of Rusholme* (London, HMSO).

Kent Education Committee. (1966) The three year course of teacher training, *Kent Education Gazette,* 47(1), June.

Kogan, M. (1971) *The politics of education: Edward Boyle and Anthony Crosland in conversation with Maurice Kogan* (London, Penguin).

Lynch, J. (1979) *The reform of teacher education in the United Kingdom* (Guildford, Society for Research in Higher Education).

Minutes of the Council of the CNAA, quoted in Minutes of Meetings 1 and 2 of the (CNAA) Special Committee on James Report, papers held at Centre for Modern Records, University of Warwick, reference DB3/98.

Parry, J. P. (1972) *The Lord James Tricycle: some notes on teacher education and training* (London, Allen & Unwin).

Plowden Report. (1967) *Primary education: report of the Central Advisory Committee for Education* (London, Department of Education and Science).

Porter, J. & Webster, R. (1972) Note of extension, in: James Report (1972) *Teacher education and training: a report by a Committee of Inquiry appointed by the Secretary of State for Education and Science, under the chairmanship of Lord James of Rusholme* (London, HMSO).

Shattock, M. (2003) *Managing successful universities* (Maidenhead, Society for Research into Higher Education and Open University Press).

Silver, H. (1975) Since James: interviews with Lord James, Roger Webster and James Porter, *Journal of Education for Teaching,* 1(1), 3–17.

Simon, B. (1975) On three insiders' views of the James Report, *Journal of Education for Teaching,* 1(2), 237–257.

Taleb, N. N. (2004) *Fooled by randomness: the hidden role of chance in life and in the markets* (London, Penguin Books).

Taleb, N. N. (2007) *Black swan: the impact of the highly improbable* (London, Allen Lane/Penguin).

Thatcher, M. (1995) *The path to power* (London, Harper Collins).

University of London Institute of Education. (1972) *The education and training of teachers: a statement by the Council of the University of London Institute of Education on the James Report* (London, Institute of Education).

Warren, C. F. (1972) The 'evidence' for James, *Education for Teaching*, 90, Spring.

Willey, F. & Maddison, R. E. (1971) *An enquiry into teacher training* (London, University of London Press).

Appendix. Adam and Eve

A lightly edited version of a paper presented by Dr Harry Judge to the Committee of Enquiry on Teacher Education and Training (James Committee) at its 14th meeting on 27/28 April 1971.

Adam played the double bass (quite well) and Eve the flute (rather better). They were sixth formers in a Comprehensive School in a prosperous London suburb, and were both being propelled towards higher education. Adam (who was at that stage happily dedicated to neither a particular career nor to Eve) was in his last few months at school and was looking forward to the undiluted study of Chemistry at York. Eve, a year younger, was looking forward—with less enthusiasm—to a final year at Amsterdam Grove and then to a course (which everyone was talking about but nobody had in fact yet taken) at Porter College. She suspected that she would like to teach but was in no great hurry to find out. Of the 16 subjects she was studying for the re-styled A level she liked best English and Geography.

As they were attending a very fine school (that is, one in which the counselors outnumbered the teachers) everything happened according to plan. ... Of Adam's life during (the next three years), no more need be said. Eve's was more original, and she greatly enjoyed it. She was able, for the two years at Porter College, to combine an extended study of English and Geography with an introductory study of education. This last did not pretend to produce teachers but it did awaken a new interest in the possibilities of teaching and allied careers. It included opportunities for studying, and being involved in the life of schools.

Eve went on playing the flute, and was interested in what happened to the rest of the wind section in the College orchestra at the end of the two years they spent together. All of them (except an unhappy French horn) were awarded the Diploma in Higher Education. A few then moved directly into employment—two into the middle reaches of educational administration, one into insurance, one into the management of British Rail, two into the Civil Service. Several (for it was a robust section that blew mightily) took themselves and their Diplomas to a Polytechnic, and studied for two or more years for an Honours degree. Even more moved into the higher reaches of advanced F[urther] E[ducation] and added to their Diplomas specialist qualifications as bi-lingual secretaries, computer programmers, Chartered librarians ...

But Eve wanted to teach, and to teach younger children. Porter College was full of people able to give good advice and to offer models. She therefore understood that, according to the book, she had completed the First Cycle of qualification, and was now eligible to enter the Second. This would last two years, and could be organised on two different patterns. The first involved a one-year full-time course (with extensive school experience), although not necessarily at her present college, followed by a one-year part-time course linked (through a Teachers' Centre) with the school at which she would by then have secured an appointment. The second version of the Cycle was, in effect, a two-year part-time course of concurrent theory and practice, but this version was based solely on the Teachers' Centre associated with the school to which appointment had been made, at the end of the First Cycle. So the first version would be familiar enough—the 1971 solution with knobs on. So to make the story a little more interesting, Eve took the second (she had other reasons too—she felt ready to be involved in work, was convinced that her chosen job could best be learned on the job, wanted to earn some money, liked the idea of settling down in one place for two years, was not excited by what she heard about school practice directed from a college base).

So she applied for a job in Gloucestershire, was appointed to the Elizabeth Aggett Primary School and assigned to the Milroy Centre in Stroud. She taught (or rather, managed the learning environment) steadily and happily for two-thirds of the week under the careful supervision of an experienced teacher-tutor, and spent one whole day at the Milroy Centre. There she received the very best professional formation—provided by a staff, some full-time and some part-time, some drawn from colleges and some from schools, some later to return to colleges and some to schools—taking part in seminars and discussions, some of them grouped round the TV programmes provided by the William Taylor Institute. She found no difficulty in relating theory to practice and felt undamaged by the absence of sociology from her diet.

Leaving the Centre one evening she noticed a double bass strapped on to an embarrassingly small car. Adam explained how he came to be there. His first degree completed, he had chosen teaching as a career, somewhat to his own surprise. The choices open to him—moving from the First into the second Cycle—were precisely the same as those presented to Eve. He had hesitated longer. Many of his contemporaries had chosen the first version, and were now spending a year either in a U[niversity] D[epartment] [of] E[ducation] or in a college [with] strong specialist provision. But he had chosen the second version and Gloucestershire, was working in a large secondary school … and was also being trained 'on the job'.

At the end of the Second Cycle, Eve collected her BA (James) and Adam his Dip. Ed. And they jointly collected a marriage certificate, thereby demonstrating among other interesting things, that the binary ditch was not impassable.

They taught in Gloucestershire for many mellow years. Eve never permanently left teaching and found no difficulty in gaining immediate access—at the Milroy Centre—to the courses and programmes she needed. Adam moved forward to a B.Ed (Webster)—entirely on the basis of work at the Centre—and later to a M.Ed after spending three Summer Schools at Porter College.

And so the years passed. In the evenings they sometimes puzzled over such insoluble questions as, 'What did our older colleagues mean by "initial training"?' or 'What were those students at Amsterdam Grove doing on that thing called "teaching practice"?', or 'Whoever wanted an old-fashioned B.Ed?' …

They lived happily … Adam did well and eventually found himself a member of a Committee on teacher education. But this was much later, and he was not depressed by the thought that every education system needs to be rebuilt for each generation.

Putting professional development centre stage

Tim Brighouse
University of London, Institute of Education, UK

All countries in the developed world aspire to ever higher standards of education and training. Clearly this depends, at least in part, on having a sufficient supply of high-quality schoolteachers. In the UK on the two occasions in the last 75 years when there were reviews of this need (the McNair report of 1944 and the James Committee of Enquiry 1971), more attention was paid to the recruitment and initial education and training of teachers than to the need for their continuous professional development. Moreover, what priority afforded to the issue was largely ignored by governments of the day whose successors have continued to pay most attention to tinkering with the supply routes and the initial training of teachers rather than their in-service professional development once they have been appointed. This paper, having accepted the crucial importance of the sustaining of teaching quality to the call for ever higher standards of pupil outcomes, sketches and evaluates the history and the present needs and proceeds to set out a menu of measures which should be considered by a third commission/committee of enquiry along the lines of its two predecessors.

The aim, now constantly given declared political priority, to achieve ever higher standards of outcome education and training is welcome to all those who have made their life's work in education in the belief that what they do makes a difference to the sort of society we have. There is a danger, however, that the urgency of the quest at a time when there is both strong public accountability and much media interest leads to a consideration of the more obvious and immediate when it comes to ensuring a sufficient and highly competent set of teachers. It is of course their efforts on a daily basis in over 400,000 classrooms in the UK which make the most contribution to the realisation of the aim for ever higher standards.

Many other government policies and actions have a bearing on the likelihood of teachers having successful interactions with their pupils. For example the present determination to rebuild or update all school buildings, the creation and appointment of many more and different sorts of support staff, the availability to this generation of teachers of an increasingly ample supply ICT equipment—all directly help the teachers in their task. So too, in the long term, will the investment in under-five pre-school provision. Regeneration, especially as it affects employment and housing, will improve the odds of inner-city teachers working successfully with their pupils. Other matters too, such as the creation of Academies or the arrangements for admission of pupils to secondary schools, influence pupil outcomes. But important though these issues are, they are not the concern of this paper which instead focuses closely on the supply and subsequent support for the teachers who make a direct difference to children's lives.

As a long-running series in the *Times Educational Supplement* testifies, we never forget teachers who made a positive difference to our lives even if they are unaware at the time—and sometimes remain so—of their impact on us. A witness statement to an enquiry[1] illustrates the beneficial 'teacher-effect' well:

> I was meant to be a welfare statistic … It is because of a teacher that I sit at this table, remember her telling us one cold, miserable day that she could not make our clothing better; she could not provide us with food, she could not change the terrible segregated conditions under which we lived. She could introduce us to the world of reading, the world of books and that's what she did.
>
> What a world! I visited Asia and Africa. I saw magnificent sunsets: I tasted exotic foods; I fell in love and danced in wonderful halls. I ran away with escaped slaves and stood beside a teenage martyr. I visited lakes and streams and composed lines of verse. I knew then that I wanted to help children do the same things. I wanted to weave magic.

The reasons for this impact vary individually both for the teacher and the taught. The teacher may have enabled us to take the first steps in what turns out to be a life-long interest or to make a breakthrough understanding of a particularly important concept or to acquire a particular skill. Whatever it is, it has proved formative. The teacher has enabled us to access something of lasting significance. If we come from families who are always providing and reinforcing positive aspirational role models, that is enough. Our families have extended our learning habits beyond the school so that we have sufficient resilience and self-confidence to withstand the mediocre or downright bad teacher. The impact of the teacher's significance is mainly cognitive. In short we do not allow school to get in the way of our education.

For children who come from unsupportive and disadvantaged homes however, where there is an absence of aspirational role models, there is an extra requirement of the teacher we remember: it lies in the affective domain. They have to convey to us their convincing belief in our capacity to learn and ultimately to be successful in that learning and to extend our horizons of what is possible in our later lives. Our insecurity both of self-esteem, when measured by the standards espoused by the school, and personal purpose is such that we appreciate the acknowledgement in the corridor, the private personal marking of our work, their illustrations of having thought about us beyond the school, their carefully selected recollections of our progress and their continuous references to their confident expectations for us. Nowadays no doubt these teachers would be considered strong in 'emotional intelligence'.

The 'significant teacher effect', whether of the first, cognitive, or second, affective sort—or indeed some combination of the two—is well summarised by Robert Fried:

> Of some of our teachers we remember their foibles and mannerisms, of others, their kindness and encouragement, or their fierce devotion to standards of work that we probably did not share at the time. And of those who inspired us most, we remember what they cared about and that they cared about us, and the person we might become. It is the quality of caring about ideas and values, this fascination with the potential for growth within people, this depth and fervour about doing things well and striving for excellence, that comes closest to what I mean in describing a 'passionate teacher'. (Fried, 2002)

It could be said that unless we encounter at least one such teacher we have not really been at school. We may have been physically present but mentally and spiritually we have been absent. Whatever the particular profile of strengths along the cognitive–affective spectrum, successful teachers have in common a third set of capacities, namely the pedagogical. This includes expertise in presenting, explaining, questioning, coaching and creating the experiences inside and beyond the classroom which will most likely lead to learning. In all these three areas—the cognitive (especially subject knowledge) the affective (especially children's development) and the pedagogical (especially the subtleties of learning as they interface with the new technologies)—the need for the teacher to be initially sufficiently equipped and subsequently and continually refreshed is significant.

It is these three areas, even if not overtly expressed and acknowledged, which will have been present on the two occasions in the last 75 years when there were clearly focused enquiries into the state of teacher education. Both reports, McNair (1944) and James (1971), however, led to greater attention being devoted to recruitment and supply routes into teaching and their pay than to their continuous professional development. The same has been true in recent years when governments have preferred to proceed from one *ad hoc* solution to another in the quest for sufficient teachers of high quality.

As this paper will shortly argue, it is time now to have a full review and to question in particular whether the balance of investment in initial supply and post-qualification professional development should not shift in favour of the latter. Let us turn briefly, though, to the two reports and subsequent developments.

The McNair report coincided with the 1944 Education Act. Its members were anxious to transform the standing of teachers as a profession and to draw a line under a period when natural routes into teaching in elementary schools still had echoes of proceeding from monitor to pupil teacher. What training there was initially came from 81 church training colleges and in the early 20th century from a similar number of maintained training colleges. After the emergency training courses for those returning from the forces after the war McNair ushered in an era where shortly (1960) three rather than two years of training became the norm for those teaching in primary schools and secondary modern schools and a degree without any specific teaching qualification was thought sufficient for those wishing to make a career in grammar schools, although some could and did take one-year post graduate diplomas in education from universities that offered them. McNair committee members could not agree and presumably spent a long time arguing whether the colleges should be put under the wings of universities or left to operate independently in loose co-operation effected by Area Training Organisations (ATOs) (Maclure, 1965). Whatever the nature of their deliberations their work had no impact on teachers' post-qualification opportunities for professional development.

The James Committee of Enquiry into teacher education, commissioned by Margaret Thatcher as Secretary of State, did give this aspect some consideration when it reported after its year's deliberations in December 1971, but its impact was inevitably constrained by context (Judge, 1984).

Both McNair and James were undertaken at a time of immense but misplaced optimism. Things were not going to turn out well. McNair suffered as the post war idealism and hope were to be heavily circumscribed and constrained by the siege economy of rationing, shortages and competing public priorities. James was undertaken when the baby boom was over and therefore when the rapid expansion of teacher training places in the ever growing number of Colleges of Education, as they were now more respectfully called after the recommendations of the Robbins committee, had to be halted and reversed. There were by then available through B.Ed. and PGCE courses more than 130,000 places annually although a combination of child birth and teacher wastage rates suggested that a figure nearer 30,000 would be sufficient. The oil crisis moreover meant that the government's response, in the unfortunately named White Paper *A Framework for Expansion*, would be largely stillborn.

Nevertheless, both McNair and James set the scene so far as general direction was concerned, for the decade or so that would follow each.

In the case of James it was not government action but local initiative that led shortly after its creation to what was arguably the first school attempt to address the induction and professional development of teachers coherently and comprehensively. Appropriately too this occurred in one of the comprehensive schools, the existence of which had first called into question the sheep and goats approach epitomised by the graduate and non-graduate entry routes to which James finally brought a resolution.

The school in question was Banbury, where Harry Judge, one of the members of James, was founding Principal. Banbury was a large (c.2000 pupils) federal comprehensive school with three 11–15 halls and an upper school for 15–19 year olds. Judge decided to appoint a Professional Tutor whose responsibility would be to ensure that newly qualified and probationary teachers should receive appropriate induction opportunities of a professional rather than administrative kind. The Professional Development Co-ordinator (the name given to the ground-breaking professional tutor post created by Judge) was also supportive of existing staff anxious to extend their initial qualifications by enrolling at a local university's department of education or otherwise to improve their skills themselves at courses and conferences run by the national subject associations or the local education authority. Simultaneously Banbury School became the first to engage on what can best be described as an action research project: money was secured from the government to employ a researcher at the nearby Oxford Department of Educational Studies to examine the relative success of 'mixed-ability' and 'setting' approaches to teaching as they were eagerly espoused and implemented in different parts of the federal Banbury School (Judge, 1984).

At the time, therefore, Banbury had in place four essential ingredients conducive to the successful development and retention of teachers: a member of staff charged with the specific responsibility to lead and be supportive of the activity within and among staff; a research focus involving many if not all the staff; a sufficient number of staff to try out and compare different ideas about curriculum and teaching with each other in a way which is impossible for many staff in small and medium sized schools; and an outstanding headteacher/principal committed as his top priority to secure, promote and sustain the intellectual curiosity of staff as a key ingredient of school success.

A further essential ingredient was created by Judge on his appointment as Director of the Oxford University Department of Educational Studies where he pioneered a model of what was subsequently to be known more widely as a 'school-based' PGCE course. Until then the pattern favoured by universities for such courses was to spend the whole of the autumn term explaining theory, philosophy and history to students before placing them for the spring term in any school which was prepared to have them even if that school was geographically remote from the university. Visits from university tutors in the spring term were inevitably few and far between: when I trained I received only one. Doubtless such arrangements had their routes in the tradition within grammar schools that graduates did not need to take a PGCE and that the pedagogical aspect of being a teacher was something you either had or did not have or might acquire by osmosis. Judge, doubtless persuaded by what he had experienced at Banbury both in its change to being a comprehensive school and its innovations, and as a member of the James Committee, wanted to change that in favour of a pattern where the school receiving the placement recognised and took on more responsibility for the initial education and training of the aspirant teacher. There needed to be clear and explicit understandings of what the university and the school would each do. Put simply the new 'school-based' model—Judge called it the 'internship' scheme using a professional medical analogy—required 'interns' to pursue a six-week intensive course at the university preparing them for what life in school would be like. This was followed by two substantial chunks in partner schools where practical education and training could be considered in a real context and where university tutors and school staff shared a partnership in the task. Instead of the school relying on, and often blaming the university department for the PGCE course, they were now actively engaged in articulating to future teachers their pedagogical rationale and in demonstrating that in action. The consequence was to stimulate the currency of its own teaching and subject knowledge. The university tutors too were often forced into demonstrating what the Council for the Accreditation of Teacher Education (CATE) called their 'recent and relevant' experience of the classroom. A model clearly based on the Oxford Internship soon became the required school-based scheme for the PGCE and partner schools were rewarded for their involvement by a share of the per-capita sum universities received for their task.

Simultaneously, Judge became involved in a further complementary initiative designed to connect serving teachers more directly to sources of intellectual stimulation and knowledge. This was to tie in the school-based internship scheme to secondment opportunities for teachers in the partner schools to the university or the local polytechnic; there to study a diploma or masters course involving curriculum, assessment or pedagogy. This was achieved by use of what was called the 'uncapped pool': that is to say expenditure incurred by any local education authority in seconding teachers on approved courses was pooled and the total annual costs then shared with some central government grant among all authorities by means of an equitable formula. Very few authorities used the scheme; they were deterred from doing so because they had to shoulder 25% of the costs of the secondment. Oxfordshire in the late 1970s and early 1980s had very constrained education budgets as school rolls fell with the decline in the birth rate and as local politicians sought to demonstrate to Margaret Thatcher's government that they were good housekeepers. The Education Committee on which Judge sat as an added member suddenly realised that the 'uncapped pool' was not such an unattractive proposition for the simple reason that it tended to be experienced and senior teachers who were seconded and their replacements were usually younger and less expensive teachers. When one added up their salary costs and the sums involved in any temporary allowances for colleagues shouldering their responsibilities in their absence on secondment, even allowing for the need to shoulder 25% of the secondee and their course costs, it was still lower than if the teacher had not gone away in the first place. In those circumstances it was cheaper for Oxfordshire to be a disproportionately large user of the 'uncapped pool'. Soon 300 teachers each year were seconded for either half a term, a whole term or a year as individuals or as groups to look at curriculum and assessment issues. A further key ingredient to creating supportive circumstances for teachers had been put in place. In short at that time—particularly in Oxfordshire, Somerset, Coventry and Leicestershire all of which authorities took full advantage of the uncapped pool and whose seconded teachers co-operated in developing a new approach to secondary assessment at age 16 through the creation of an Oxford Certificate of Educational Achievement (OCEA) and the development of 'Thinking Skills' in schools—there was a potentially powerful arrangement to stimulate existing teachers while managing the debilitating effects of falling rolls. In Oxfordshire it was especially effective since all schools had been early adopters of the Banbury Professional Tutor model and were involved with in the 'Internship' scheme.

In 1989, however, two events conspired to bring parts of this unprecedented and propitious set of circumstances to a sudden end. The government introduced a new, and minutely centrally prescribed, National Curriculum, which removed the requirement for teachers to be creative about the curriculum, and—even more significantly—it discontinued the arrangements for the 'uncapped pool'. Moreover, Local Management of Schools (LMS) meant that LEAs would no longer have money to run professional development courses other than those which ensured that teachers followed to the letter the centrally prescribed details of the new curriculum. Secondments were discontinued. It would be up to schools themselves individually to decide how to spend the totality of their recurrent budget. Unsurprisingly continuous professional development was low on their priority list for two principal reasons. First, the rules of LMS required that the school had to carry the real rather than the average cost of teachers' salaries: this meant in practice that schools with high salary costs had to shed expensive, and usually more experienced teachers while others, with low salary costs, succumbed to the natural temptation to appoint more teachers and thereby reduce class size—always regarded by schools, whatever the research evidence to the contrary, as the surest way to improve standards. Secondly, the schools with their new financial freedoms received no guidance to protect monies for the professional development of teachers. On the contrary, the introduction of the five so-called 'Baker' or in-service training days as part of the teachers' contract encouraged them to think that all that needed to be done could be accommodated then. (It is worth noting in passing that there has been no serious study of the consequences of that change but it is worth noting that in the decade leading to 1989 the performance of Oxfordshire secondary schools had risen much more sharply than and was ahead of the national average—17% to 37% as opposed to 20% to 35%— whereas by 2006 the reverse was the case.)

Since 1988 there have been many *ad hoc* changes to initial teacher education but very little attention to and expenditure on teachers' subsequent professional development. An examination of what has happened when coupled with an analysis of what has been described above, however, lends support in its lack of coherence to the need now for a review along the lines of James.

For many years leading up to and beyond James, the B.Ed had become a major route into teaching based mainly on the old teacher training colleges. Designed as an optional fourth year after the three-year teacher training course, it was the natural way to realise the vision of an all graduate profession. The cut-back of initial training numbers during the late 1970s and 1980s from c.130,000 to c.30,000 a year was effected by closing colleges rather than university departments. The number of B.Ed entrants declined naturally; and as the remaining colleges of education attached themselves to universities it became more common for those deciding at age 18 that they definitely wanted to teach to take three-year honours undergraduate courses in which Education was the principal discipline of their BA or BSc rather than their B.Ed Initial professional qualification could then follow through the PGCE.

The main sources of new teachers are now therefore via the school-based PGCE, led either by a university or by a Schools Consortium for Initial Teacher Training (SCITT) in partnership with a university. These two variants account for c.27,000 of the c.34,500 annual training places approved by a national quango, the TDA, until recently called the Teacher Training Agency. (This body was originally created to promote teaching as a profession as we continue to experience teacher shortages either acutely in areas of high housing costs, or particularly and generally in what are called the shortage subjects.) The balance (of c.7,500) is taken up by what are called Employment Based Routes. There are four such routes, of which two are the most common. Around 1400 teachers each year, mainly in large cities, especially London, come from overseas from countries whose qualifications need to be recognised as appropriate to the UK schooling system's needs. Based in schools these teachers are either assessed or provided with bespoke part-time training courses, There is also a steady stream (c.5,000) of teachers through the 'graduate training programme' (GTP) for graduates who train on the job and receive a lower wage or are self-funded for a year. There are two other smaller initial programmes. The (c.250) registered teacher programme is for those who have satisfactorily completed two years of a three-year degree course and wish to complete the final year while learning to teach, with appropriate training on the job. The final, equally small scheme is 'Teach First'. Based on 'Teach for America' the programme is targeted at good graduates from the best universities who are thinking of a career in commerce, finance or industry but whose sense of public service might be enlisted to teach for two years in an inner city school before embarking on their chosen career. Their initial training is minimal—a short course during the summer prior to placement in school—and at the end of their first year they receive QTS.

The problem with this route is often thought to lie with the fact that after two years these new teachers are scheduled to leave the profession. But wastage rates have also been high through other routes. For at least 30 years it has generally been accepted that of those who commence training in the UK more than one in three is not in school five years later and of those who are newly qualified in school and actually start their teaching career one in five has left within five years. More research needs to be done on this matter and the most reliable figure is probably that of the House of Commons Select Committee (2004) which 'thought that as many as 50% of those embarking on initial training were not teaching five years later'.[2]

It is at least arguable that an alternative strategy would be to shift the balance of the initial training routes and reduce the long-term costs by reforming the PGCE along the lines of 'Teach First'. (One of the interesting early features of that scheme is that as many as 50% of those reaching the supposed end of the two years they have committed to teaching then continue in teaching. Of course it is too early to be sure whether that's a reliable guide to the number who will make a substantially longer commitment to teaching, but it is not at first glance less cost effective than the more expensive PGCE route.) If the PGCE were to be remodelled along the lines of 'Teach First' it would not necessarily improve wastage rates of course. One of the interesting features of 'Teach First', however, is that the initial training immersion is seen by those taking it as likely to be of value in some of their ultimate jobs in business and the wider public and private sector. Presumably these are the same employment sectors as those leaving the profession after pursuing the conventional but more expensive PGCE. In short it would be better to acknowledge that whatever the model of initial education and training at least some of it has and always will be of relevance to other employment sectors.

Another future route must surely grow out of the registered teacher programme where, as has been noted, graduates can complete their degree while working in a school and acquiring QTS. The introduction of foundation degrees will mean many more deciding during that period that teaching is their preferred profession. Both routes will still require schools to take on a shared responsibility for the task of training teachers, a process which has been beneficial to a school's more explicit focus on improving teaching and learning.

These arrangements and shifts of emphasis would still require teachers to demonstrate on assessment that they satisfy the competences demanded by the TDA. As they are set out for various stages in a teacher's career leading to Advanced Skills status, or indeed en route for headship via the NPQH, however, present arrangements overlook the need to create a coherent set of opportunities and entitlements that will both help teachers acquire the competences and serve as a means of keeping people within the profession for longer. At present there is a rapidly approaching problem of securing a sufficient supply of headteachers—the so-called 'succession crisis' (see National College for School Leadership, 2007). Teacher shortages in mathematics, design technology, science and even English remain chronic. When asked, teachers find non-salary matters key to their decisions on where, and indeed, whether they teach (Moon, 2007). In short there is much greater need to spend money on the professional development of teachers when qualified.

Teachers of the sort outlined at the beginning of this paper flourish best when four needs are met. First they thrive on *responsibility*; that is to be recognised as the trusted expert and to be allowed to lead on some aspect of teaching, assessment, curriculum or school organisational matter. Secondly they flourish when they enjoy *permitting circumstances*; that is most often affected by the leadership of the department, the phase or the school in which they teach. It needs to be a place where they are encouraged to develop, take risks and not be blamed and where they are surrounded by habits best suited to encouraging professional dialogue which stimulates and excites them about their present and especially their future contribution to education. Thirdly they need like anyone else, *respect and recognition*; pay and conditions are important but so too is appreciation of their efforts when it is deserved in the school, the local community and more widely. Fourthly they need *new experiences*; opportunities to see others doing similar and different jobs on a regular basis, access to subject association meetings and courses, conferences, opportunities to study and to research, reflect and adjust their practice.

Arguably it is the satisfaction of these four needs of serving teachers which will both contribute most to their retention for longer periods and importantly to school improvement. (Judith Little has set out one of the best guides to a recipe for school success when she described successful schools or departments where teachers *talked* about teaching; *observed* each other teach; planned monitored and evaluated their work *together*; and *taught each other* [Bird & Little, 1986].)

So what should the ingredients be of investment in the continous professional development of teachers? Certainly harking back to a golden age of term or year secondments is impractical and fails to acknowledge changes since. We could never afford such a programme and it would make the present teacher supply crisis worse. Moreover some of the changes that have occurred since provide pointers to the way forward in professional development, just as we have argued above they do to the future of initial education and training.

School-based attention to the issue now provides many examples of practices that could be established more widely. For example some schools have regular weekly or fortnightly sessions of an hour or so devoted to teachers teaching each other. Another school uses one of its five 'Baker'/occasional days each year on focused and purposeful visits in twos and threes to other schools which are in session and whose data show them to be very comparable in terms of pupil prior attainment and socio-economic characteristics at intake but performing differently at outcome. Yet other schools variously have thorough induction for all staff or as a matter of course seek the views of newly arrived staff on good practices they have seen elsewhere. A few pay for the first year's subscription to a professional subject association. Most have some form of structured professional review, albeit sometimes unhelpfully called 'performance management'. Residential opportunities for whole staff development and school improvement are now often school organised and 'partnerships of schools' in loose federations or collegiates[3] have yielded some examples of what the participants see as enriched professional development. Most schools now have a senior member of the leadership team whose responsibility it is to lead professional development to a degree undreamed of when Judge's Banbury took its first tentative steps in 1971.

Beyond the school too there have been changes which provide pointers for the future. The Open University has become a main provider both of initial teacher training through its part-time PGCE and, more importantly, of post-qualification learning for teachers through its MA courses. The Open University was also the first to try to harness the new technologies through its 'teachandlearn' net venture which faltered only for the lack of an adequate and sustainable financial model. Some of the major charitable foundations[4] have also provided models of bursary opportunities for teachers for action research and further training.

Successive governments, however, have given the further professional development of teachers intermittent and essentially *ad hoc* attention. Even when they tried to arrange something more coherent in 2002, it became the first cut a year later when it had to accommodate the unanticipated high cost of a pay deal coupled with changes in the local management of schools.

We now need some review not only of what schools themselves do, for example the proportion of the school budget the best of them spend on professional development and the most promising in-school practice, but also of what governments do. For example, is there a case for every teacher being entitled to £2500 for every five years they spend in one institution to buy time off-timetable to pursue some sort of research or further training? Should that be accompanied by tax breaks for the cost of approved further degrees and/or salary recognition obtaining them? Should schools be asked to match the £2,500 grant from their own professional development budget and should OFSTED report and judge the adequacy of professional development in school? What are the most cost-effective models of initial teacher education? What is the role of higher education—and the Open University in particular—in both? Should the government fund something like 'teachandlearn.net'? The questions even when not rhetorical are many. The circumstances in which the profession now operates are very different from the recent past. The new technologies have meant that the teacher is no longer the prime imparter of knowledge. Learning barriers also can be substantially reduced by the use of the technologies as a tool. The expansion in the numbers and role of support staff has in turn changed the role of teachers too.

What is now needed 35 years on from James and over 50 since McNair is another tightly timed committee of enquiry into teacher education. It should have an open brief. The government, however, might break with tradition and encourage it to consider an expanded and reformed budget to guide its recommendations. It might also be encouraged to open with a review of what has and has not worked and what is the practice in other educationally more successful countries such as Finland and all the countries which by international comparison do better for their student populations than we do.

Notes

1. Anon. Evidence to the American Commission into state of Education (1999).
2. *Education Guardian* (11 September 2007).
3. Weston-super-Mare has a thriving partnership of secondary schools which organises such professional development: there are many others in for example Dorset and Birmingham.
4. Gatsby teacher fellowships; The Gatsby Foundation, London.

References

Bird, T. & Little, J. W. (1986) How schools organise the teaching occupation, *The Elementary School Journal,* 86(4), 493–511.

Fried, R. (2002) *The passionate teacher: a practical guide* (Boston, Beacon Press).

Judge, H. (1984) *A generation of schooling: English secondary schools since 1944* (Oxford, Oxford University Press).

Maclure, J. S. (1965) *Educational documents: England and Wales 1816–1963* (London, Chapman & Hall).

Moon, R. E. (2007) *Teaching matters: the recruitment, employment and retention of teachers* (London, Politaea).

National College for School Leadership. (2007) *The succession crisis* (Nottingham, NCSL).

Teacher education at Oxford University: James is alive but living in Karachi

Richard Pring
University of Oxford, UK

The arguments at Oxford about the start of teacher education within the University have been repeated many times and in many ways, not least in the 1972 James Committee. The strong advocacy there for much greater attention to, and investment in, continuing professional development may not have won the day in England, but, through the influence of Harry Judge, it has had an impact in the development of the Institute for Educational Development at the Aga Khan University, with which the Oxford Department remains closely associated.

Part 1

Introduction

Teacher education and training has a chequered history, reflected not least in its history within the University of Oxford, but also elsewhere as is apparent from the various contributions to this volume. Does the well-prepared teacher require no more than a good education in the subject which he or she is to teach? Or does not the future teacher need also a theoretical understanding of educational practice? Or does the teacher require a period of professional training in addition to the acquisition of 'subject knowledge' and in addition to the educational theory? Or ought the emphasis upon professional training be shifted to a later stage in the teacher's career when it can be built on experience? And, if so, should such training be coterminous with the acquisition of subject knowledge?

In effect, then, there would seem to be four possibilities, which in one way or another have shaped the debate about the preparation of teachers, not least at Oxford from the prolonged period of the birth of educational studies at the University in the 1890s to the present day.

The first possibility is that there is no need for professional training for the able and well educated young person (that is, let the university simply make sure that the future teacher knows his or her teaching subject). The second possibility is that there is need for professional training in addition to the subject knowledge, but that it should be undertaken elsewhere—in a professional centre or in the schools themselves. The third possibility is that the balance of professional training between initial and later periods of the teaching career should be skewed to the latter. Yet a fourth possibility is that there is need for professional training, but that it should be stiffened with a theoretical perspective and research base, and that therefore it should be the responsibility of the university, albeit in partnership with schools (the future teacher needs theory as well as practice), to impart that theory. Of course, there could be many variations on the last possibility, depending on the nature of the partnership and the relationship between the theoretical and practical perspectives.

The solutions have been various, and the arguments continue—both as to the nature of educational studies (and even as to the appropriateness of 'educational studies' as the title of a university department) and to appropriate place for such studies (whatever their nature) to be undertaken. The arguments were well rehearsed in Oxford when it embarked upon its preparation of teachers in 1892, as was reflected in the evidence given to the Bryce Commission of 1895; they were rehearsed again for the McNair Report in 1944, and again by the James Report in 1972, and they continue to be rehearsed in the era of the Research Assessment Exercise.

Should Oxford University train teachers?

Oxford has throughout been party to these debates, and therefore it is useful to begin the story there—not least because, in later years, Harry Judge, both before and after he was appointed to the University, was a significant and creative contributor to these debates (and not only in Britain).

The University established an Elementary Day Training College in October 1892 at No. 19 Holywell Street—partly because (at least, so it is surmised) Cambridge had started one a year earlier. The students attending the College would enter the University through the 'Non-Collegiate Delegacy', founded in 1868 for the purpose of enabling people, in particular poor men otherwise unable to attend, to enter Oxford and thereby to gain access to the professions (law, the Church, medicine). Hence, with regard to the preparation for teaching, what was being proposed was a sort of 19th-century two part B.Ed—three years' subject knowledge and one year's professional training.

However, the debate which preceded the establishment of the Day Training College showed some reluctance on the part of the University, since the good teacher was seen to require only to be well educated, the practical and professional side being left to experience under a wise head teacher. Mr Raleigh of All Souls explained to the Bryce Commission in 1895:

> It is not the office of the University to train men for teaching, or for any other profession. ... His special training must be left to those who are engaged in professional work. ...

> Almost any honours man will make a good teacher, if he is conscientious, and if he has the luck to fall into the hands of a good head teacher. (Bryce Commission, 1895)

It should, however, be added in parenthesis that even Mr Raleigh admitted (no doubt reluctantly) that 'we might of course (one day) have a professor of education'.

However, Mr Raleigh's reservations were not universally agreed with. That is, not everyone believed that all that was necessary for a person to teach was that he should be a 'good honours man'. Something more was required, and that 'more' was some theory. Miss Maitland, Principal of Somerville, also in evidence to the Bryce Commission, expressed the belief that:

> the business of the University is to give instruction in the theory only. The practice, *once the theory is understood*, should be acquired elsewhere. (Bryce Commission, 1895, emphasis added)

This separation of theory from practice was endorsed by the first Principal of the Day Training College, Dr Jackson of Exeter College:

> Universities should provide for courses on theory and the half-fledged teachers should thus be scattered to the schools where arrangements for practical training should be made, this being no concern of the University lectures on theory. (Bryce Commission, 1895)

Indeed, Herbert Warren, President of Magdalen, sharing the sentiments of Mr Raleigh, believed that the theory most suited to school teaching was to be found in Plato's *Republic* and Aristotle's *Politics* and *Ethics*, and therefore that, though the teaching of theory was valuable, the practical skill of school teaching would in effect be acquired easily by the well educated person, requiring only abbreviated courses in educational theory.

> ... a young man who has passed through an English public school, more particularly if he has been ... a prefect ... has had experience in keeping order and maintaining discipline ... Thus the average Oxford man, more especially the classical student, ought not to require so long an additional training, either in theory or in practice, as is sometimes necessary for students elsewhere. (Bryce Commission, 1895)

Not everyone, however, agreed either with Mr Raleigh that the well educated 'honours man' without theory or practice could adequately manage or with Miss Maitland that the 'honours man' with appropriate theory was sufficient. A third way of seeing things was put to the Bryce Commission by the Oxford dons. Mr Barnett of Wadham saw professional preparation to require:

> The self-critical habit of mind, practical interest in the discovery of method developed by the discipline of teaching under criticism. (Bryce Commission, 1895)

Mr Haverfield of Christ Church spoke of the need to 'get the future teacher thinking about teaching'. And Mr Sidgwick of Corpus Christi put forward the case that the business of the University was the training of the teacher as a whole—instruction in the theory and history of education, certainly, but also in the practice of teaching and in an apprenticeship to schools which would be in some relationship with the university.

Those who believed that universities had a role in teacher education, that such a role included subject knowledge, theory of education and some formation of practice through critical reflection on practice, won the debate. In November 1896, Congregation voted for an examination in the theory, history and practice of education. It should be mentioned, however, that such a revolutionary advance, despite the reservations of so many dons, was attributed to:

> the imposing presence of a number of unknown voters who had been attracted to the University by the prospect of enjoying lunch first and a little irresponsible legislation afterwards. (Bryce Commission, 1895)

Therefore, in concluding this section, we see, in the contributions from Oxford to the Bryce Commission, differently perceived dimensions of university involvement in the education and training of teachers: general education alone; general education plus theory; general education plus theory and practice in collaboration with the schools. Over subsequent years, there have been many variations on each of these three components and on their interrelationship. And if, until the 1970s, the emphasis was on 'theory' at the expense of practical know-how (the 'half-fledged teachers being scattered to the schools'), that would be because Oxford was part of a national movement to make educational studies more academically respectable.

Academic respectability

The fears of many expressed in contributions to the Bryce Commission were never far beneath the surface in subsequent years, especially the fear of the possible erosion of academic respectability once the Universities got involved in practical competence. Put in more modern terms, can a University department of educational studies excel in research whilst being immersed in classroom practice? In such practical competence they had no expertise, and indeed nor should they have—practical knowledge is vastly different from academic enquiry. Therefore, much of teacher training took place in *training* colleges under the loose tutelage of University Institutes of Education, including that established at Oxford University, following the McNair Report of 1944.

The position changed following the Robbins Report of 1963, when the expansion of higher education involved the upgrading of teaching to an all graduate profession. The two year *training* course became a three year *education* course—designating a broader preparation for teaching, one in which the future teacher would have a wider 'cognitive perspective' on the practice of teaching. The introduction of the B.Ed degree—'ordinary' after three years, 'honours' after four—necessarily drew the colleges closer to the universities and created the need for greater 'academic respectability' for the studies of education.

For many, that academic rigour was sorely needed. At the Hull conference of the Association of Teachers in Colleges and Departments of Education, in 1964, Professor Richard Peters, recently appointed to the Chair of Philosophy of Education at the University of London Institute of Education, referred to the 'undifferentiated mush' which passed for educational theory—and in that he echoed the sentiments of the Reverend Mr Pope of the Oxford University Students' Delegacy, who, 70 years earlier,

> had the misfortune to hear one or two lectures on the art of teaching delivered to elementary schoolmasters and [whose recollection was] that they consisted of a mass of common sense expressed in very elaborate language.

The Hull conference was a turning point. Teaching should be served by rigorous studies in the philosophy, psychology, sociology and history of education—the foundation disciplines—and thenceforth arose theoretical perspective sustained by the B.Ed. degree examinations and reflected in specialised journals and publications (for example, the various series in the 'foundation disciplines', published by Routledge and Kegan Paul).

However, not everyone thought that all was well. Was not academic rigour purchased at the expense of practical relevance? What was the connection between the theory, thus strengthened, and the practice which was so messy and difficult to capture? What is the connection between the theory or 'knowledge that', which the universities were good at, and the practice or 'knowledge how', which school teachers were to be good at?

Principles of James Report and the Oxford Internship Scheme

The significance of the James Report is that it put forward a solution to the problems which seemed to have baffled the profession, universities and the government for so long. It proposed three cycles: the first being that in which the future teacher acquires subject knowledge—for example, in an undergraduate degree; the second being that in which the future teacher is professionally trained, acquiring the practical know-how to convey that knowledge and to create the conditions for its transmission; the third, being the continuing professional development of the teacher once established within the profession. The first cycle takes place within a university setting; the second, preferably in professional centres whether within or without universities; the third, which would occur once in every seven years (or, where possible, every five years) would be where the teacher felt most benefit would be gained, including further study at university where that subject knowledge might be enhanced. But the three cycles, to obtain coherence, did require more fruitful relationships between universities and 'professional centres' which were likely to be the very great number of training colleges (or colleges of education, a significant change in nomenclature following the Robbins Report in 1963) or indeed the 'field-based' Teachers' Centres soon to flourish across the country. The role of the professionally prepared teachers in the school to help implement cycles two and three underpinned the thinking of the Committee.

That is a very rough and ready summary, for both first and second cycle could be taken in the Colleges of Education which were able to offer the new B.Ed. degree which combined first and second cycles. None the less the concept of the 'professional centre', howsoever blurred it became, was still embedded in the practice. Colleges were primarily concerned with professional development, and would 'house' a suitable place, resources and expertise for the teacher on the third cycle to gain the support required for his or her professional improvement. That expertise would include teachers in schools who would be attached to such 'professional centres'. The goal of the second and third cycle was essentially that of improved professional practice in schools—not 'more theory' unless it could be demonstrated that the 'more theory' was integral to improved learning.

Furthermore, such professional centres, whether set within or set without the universities, included Teachers' Centres, generally 'owned' by the local education authority, but run by teachers and for teachers. These Centres were particularly significant after the establishment of the Schools Council in 1964, an attempt to democratise decision making about the curriculum in schools, as teachers, as part of their professional development, were seen as 'curriculum creators', not as 'curriculum deliverers'. Teachers' Centres were a crucial part of curriculum renewal and teacher development in the 1970s and early 1980s—a model of the 'third cycle' of the James Report. And there was there, too, an integration of the University and the schools in the development of a tradition of action research into the advancement of knowledge about the practice of teaching, led in particular by the newly established Centre for Applied Research in Education at the University of East Anglia (CARE).

In many respects, the principles of the James Committee were alive and well, particularly in Oxford itself, as Harry Judge, by then the Director of the Department of Educational Studies—inheritor of the Oxford debate about the role of the University in the preparation of teachers and interpreter of the James Report to which he made a major contribution—set about putting those principle into practice. At least in Oxford James would be found alive and well.

The Oxford Model Internship

The Internship Model required a partnership between the university, the local education authority and the schools, in which the continuing professional development of the teachers (funded by the LEA) would be integral to their partnership role in the preparation of the next generation of teachers. The principles of the model might be summarised as follows:

(i) the training of the future teachers takes place within a partnership between University and schools;
(ii) each brings to that training distinctive kinds of knowledge: the contextual, craft and professional knowledge of the teacher, and the research based knowledge of the University;
(iii) the setting for the bringing together of these two types of knowledge is the school, and therefore the university tutor works with the teachers in a joint programme in the school itself;
(iv) the school, therefore, becomes 'a training school'—a 'professional centre'—with a substantial number of 'interns' (eight to twelve) attached to it, each mentored by the subject specialist and each participating in the broader analysis of the context of learning under the 'professional tutor';
(v) there is a recognition that the interns, through the programme, need to develop their own teaching style and their own educational thinking on important matters;

(vi) in doing so, the interns need to test their ideas within the wider learning group of interns, mentors, professional tutors and university staff—against, in other words, the contextualised experience of the teachers, the growing knowledge of the other interns and the decontextualised knowledge and research introduced by the university tutor.

Key therefore to the Internship Model is the recognition of the professional knowledge of the teacher and of the key role, as part of his or her own professional learning, in what the James Report would refer to as the 'second cycle'. Central, too, is the distinctive roles which the university and the schools play in the second and third cycles. James was alive and well, but living in Oxford.

Part II

The Aga Khan University and the Institute for Educational Development

The Aga Khan University was established in the early 1980s in Karachi, Pakistan. It was, in many senses, unique as a university foundation. From the beginning it was intended to be 'world class', and yet it did not start with the subject or mission which one would normally associate with a world class university—the study of history, of law, of sciences, or of theology. The creation of the university was primarily to meet the social problems of a developing country where many were deprived of basic necessities for a fulfilling life—health care, medical treatment and education. These services required professional knowledge and preparation, albeit in the context of appropriate research. The first courses therefore were in community health care, quickly followed by the establishment of a medical school. Already there was an underlying conception of the relation of theory to practice. Theory cannot be developed independently of practical involvement—the 'making sense of the situation' which one is in and experiencing. Theory (often bad theory) is embodied in practice, rather than being developed independently of, and then applied to, practice. And both theoretical development and practical improvement go hand in hand. If it is bad theory, then that will be revealed in the critical analysis of the theoretical underpinnings, rarely acknowledged, of the practice.

It made sense, therefore, to advance the practical interests of the university in social improvement to the field of education, for indeed the improvement in medical welfare and social well-being depended upon a more educated public.

Subsequently, therefore, the Aiglemont Secretariat of His Highness the Aga Khan established a Task Force, which, in October 1989, produced a Report on Education in Pakistan (The Aga Khan Institutions and Teachers in Pakistan, 1989). At the heart of the Report was the belief that:

> the education of all children in Pakistan depends on the improvement of the performance and the elevation of dignity of teachers, and further that such an improvement in turn depends upon the creation of a network of teacher development, dispersed throughout Pakistan but linked with a centre of excellence of international quality. (p. 2)

In so doing, the Task Force Report argued strongly against a traditional university faculty. Rather, what was needed were professional centres, located within, or at least linked to, a university so as to ensure a close connection with research into policy and into field-based teacher development. School improvement depended on teacher improvement, and teacher improvement required professional centres within which the teachers could reflect upon practice—systematically, in the light of evidence and in the light of whatever research had to say.

Already there are to be detected shades of the James Report—the 'elevation of the dignity of teachers', 'the network of teacher development', and yet the link to the kind of knowledge which usually only a university would provide. But, further, this would build on initiatives already underway, especially the field based teacher development centres within the Aga Khan Development Network—for example, the Professional Development Centres (PDCs) in Gilgit and the teacher resource centre in Karachi.

There are good reasons why there should be shades of James, for the key papers which led to the development of the Institute of Educational Development were written by Harry Judge, a member of the Task Group. The work of the Professional Development Centre was to draw upon the example of clinical training in medicine.

> First and foremost it locates the task of teacher training and development in the context of real schools (rather than of lecture based theory) and exploits the expertise both of practising teachers of high quality and of educational researchers and scholars. Dominant in the PDS (Professional Development Schools) are master teachers (or clinical instructors) who are trained to act as mentors to the less experienced teachers who attend the PDS for continuous periods of about eight weeks ... The intensive work undertaken by those teachers is overseen by the IED and in most cases contributes to credits for degrees in education now awarded by the Aga Khan University. (Judge, p. 2)

To help with this, the Aga Khan University would establish partnerships with universities of international repute which shared this James-like vision. One of the two universities chosen was that of Oxford, and in the last ten years or so there has developed a radical approach to the professional development of teachers—assisted by Oxford University and influenced by the principles of the Internship Model. The Professional Development Centre in the IED, and also in Gilgit, Northern Pakistan, provide the contexts in which the visiting teachers are supported by master teachers, who themselves had most probably been once upon a time visiting teachers. These in turn are supported by permanent staff of the University, engaged in research into field based training—some of whom were themselves recruited from the Master Teachers members of the IED faculty had received their doctorates from Oxford University. Karachi.

As explained by Fauzia Shamim and Anjum Halai (Shamim & Halai, 2006), the essential characteristics of the programme were:

- a focus on whole school improvement led by the 'master teachers' who have been trained to lead in this through their continuing professional development—leading to an M.Ed degree;
- collaboration between such 'master teachers' and teachers in the associated schools who were less advanced in experience and competence;
- a focus on action research as a way of promoting both the collaboration and the critical analysis of the assumptions behind the practices.

Indeed, Mr Barnett of Wadham would have been happy to witness what he had advocated for Oxford so long ago, which was integral to the third cycle of the James Report, which received a particular and influential form in the Oxford Internship Model and which, due partly to the contribution of Oxford, was to flourish in Karachi; namely, a professional preparation requiring 'the self-critical habit of mind, practical interest in the discovery of method developed by the discipline of teaching under criticism'.

It is truly the case that James is alive and well, and living in Karachi.

References

The Aga Khan Institutions and Teachers in Pakistan (1989) *Report of the Task Force on education in Pakistan,* (Aiglemont, France, Aga Khan).

Bryce Commission (1895–96) *The Royal Commission on Secondary Education 1894–95 (Bryce Commission) Report* (London, HMSO).

Shamim, F. & Halai, A. (2006) Developing professional development teachers, in: I. Farah, & B. Jaworski (eds) *Partnerships in educational development* (Didcot, Oxford, Symposium Books).

A view from within: revisiting Harry Judge's *American Graduate Schools of Education: a view from abroad*

Patricia Albjerg Graham
Harvard University, USA

Twenty-five years ago when Harry Judge published *American Graduate Schools of Education: a view from abroad*, he referred to his subject as a 'puzzle'. These institutions were in the midst of a transition from a focus upon the education of academically talented children mostly from affluent backgrounds to the schooling of children of disparate academic abilities often from non-affluent backgrounds. Further, many were ambivalent toward schooling as a focus for their schools of education, preferring more expansive definitions of education which minimised issues of schooling. Finally, most were strengthening their research capacities with infusions of disciplinary traditions and methodologies. Policy was emerging as a new specialty. The present emphasis, barely evolving when Judge wrote his book, now has schooling (particularly for the poor), and improvement of the practice of education, at the forefront. These shifting emphases have pushed educational researchers to investigate different questions, and their inquiry has been improved by the earlier disciplinary infusions. The evolution of these institutions remains much slower than the changing taste of the public, a circumstance that preserves much of the best of the past but does not incorporate rapidly enough new concerns, leaving the institutions subject to considerable criticism.

Introduction

Twenty years after the Sputnik had alerted Americans and others to the Soviet Union's scientific prowess, British historian and educator, Harry Judge, agreed in 1977 with a leading US philanthropy, the Ford Foundation, to undertake a study of American graduate schools of education. He concentrated his analysis upon those located in eminent research universities, thereby excluding nearly all the institutions that prepared most of the teachers and administrators for the American schools. His decision to concentrate upon this smaller group, however, allowed him to focus upon the debates that were beginning to roil the waters of all professional education. The storm has not yet abated.

Five years later, in 1982, The Ford Foundation published Judge's insightful analysis as *American Graduate Schools of Education: a view from abroad.* Now, twenty-five years later, the issue Judge identified remains one that graduate schools of education in major research universities continue to confront: the dilemma of uniting theory and practice in order both to understand and to improve education. Attention to increasing student learning in schools has waxed and waned in importance in these institutions but at the moment it is at an all time high, largely because both the American public and, surprisingly, the federal government say this is what they want from schooling.

The élite schools of education that Judge examined traditionally have been especially concerned about the schools that prepared the students who were likely to be their undergraduates, namely academically successful youngsters who frequently lived in affluent communities. Typically these are the children who attended their 'lab schools'. Today, however, these same institutions recognise that the national demand has shifted from the academically strong to the academically weak student. Significant academic learning for everybody is a novelty for schools, for society and also for schools of education. This is the transition Judge foresaw in his 1982 essay.

Judge was prescient in recognising the shifting priorities among American graduate schools of education in research universities in the late 1970s. He opens his volume with a description of the 'puzzle' he encountered as he worked on his book. Why, he wondered, did these schools of education 'occupy so unclear and uncomfortable a position, both in the world of research universities and in other fields'? As an historian, Judge undoubtedly understood that studying an issue in the present limits one's perspective. The past seems much clearer than the future.

Research university Graduate Schools of Education: 1957 to 1982

Fifty years ago Americans perceived the principal educational need of the nation to be the preparation of an academic élite that would allow the US to compete successfully internationally, particularly with the perceived Russian superiority in science, thought to be a distinct threat at the height of the Cold War. Intense criticism of American schools for their flaccid curriculum, based on notions of progressive education delivered to aspiring teachers and administrators in schools of education throughout the country, rocked the popular press in magazines and in books. Rudolf Flesch (1955) asked why Johnny can't read. Hyman Rickover (1962) asserted Swiss schools are better than ours. Arthur Bestor (1953) alleged American schools were an 'educational wasteland' and concluded in the second volume that what was needed was 'restoration of learning' (1955).

Professors in major schools of education found themselves grappling with this assault on their enterprise. Many of the Teachers College, Columbia professors were nationally recognised as leading spokesmen for 'progressive education' which sought to unleash children's creativity, free them from the bondage of a rigid curriculum, and support their development in many areas. At its best it was wonderful both for the children and for the teachers. Rarely was it at its best, and for the rest it collapsed into 'life adjustment education': 20% of the children were prepared for college; 20% for vocational training; and the remaining 60% for 'life adjustment'.

The external critics decried the life adjustment curriculum and the academic performance of the students enrolled in it. Yet again the public critics were setting the priorities for education, not the educators themselves as had been briefly the case during the Depression and the Second World War when public attention shifted away from education. In this vacuum the educators, for once, had led the national discussion about education. In the post-war years when the birth rate soared, reaching its peak in 1957, quality of schooling emerged as a major issue for the country. This was particularly true for the rising middle class, who joined the critics in their attacks on schools that they believed were not preparing their children adequately for the bright future expected of them.

In the face of the virulent external criticism of the schools and the schools of education that prepared their teachers and administrators, some post-war professors of education caught the wave of reform and redirected their attention to topics deemed more prestigious both to their colleagues in the university's departments of humanities and social sciences as well as to the critics calling for better preparation of an academic elite. This development took two principal forms: research in education that was tied to canons of the disciplines and preparation of teachers and administrators principally for schools serving affluent, academically-able students. What Judge observed in his visits in the late 1970s was the approaching senescence of these initiatives.

Teachers College, Columbia, again provided a leader of the new effort in educational research, namely Lawrence Cremin, whom the New York Times dubbed the leader of the 'Young Turks'. Cremin studied in the 1940s at Teachers College with George S. Counts, a leading progressive educator who had challenged his colleagues to develop a social vision for progressive education, a task they did not fulfil. Cremin, however, believed that the future for education lay in closer alignment with colleagues in the disciplines, and he undertook to change his department of 'Social and Philosophical Foundations of Education' to one (termed 'Philosophy and Social Sciences' in 1965) in which faculty trained in philosophy, history, sociology, political science, anthropology, and economics applied their disciplinary knowledge to the study of education. This infusion of the methodological canons of the disciplines has improved educational research enormously. It has not, however, raised the status of education professors among their disciplinary colleagues, undoubtedly a subsidiary objective. Ultimately economists seem to have found education the most interesting, as evidenced by the more than one hundred members of the National Bureau of Economics Research group on education, most of whom are located in economics departments.

Also in 1965 Cremin organised the National Academy of Education, an honorary society for educators. Its organisation demonstrated Cremin's interests in academic disciplines applied to education with four of five sections of the Academy grouped by discipline (i.e. Section I was History and Philosophy) and only the fifth (and smallest), termed 'general', included distinguished practitioners. Only five of the founding members held sole positions in schools of education; the remainder were in arts and science departments solely or held joint appointments between education and an arts and science department. None was a woman or a person of colour. Such was the triumph in the minds of élite educators of disciplinary knowledge both over issues of educational practice and over the educational needs of the poor and minority students. The educational interests of the nation that year, however, focused upon passage of the first major federal aid to schools, the Elementary and Secondary Education Act, which sent funds to school districts with concentrations of low income families, and upon the school desegregation cases emerging eleven years after the Brown decision in which the US Supreme Court declared racial segregation in public schools unconstitutional.

Cremin's definition of education was broad: 'the deliberate, systematic, and sustained effort to transmit, evoke, or acquire knowledge, values, attitudes, skills, and sensibilities, as well as any learning that results from that effort, direct or indirect, intended or unintended' (Cremin 1980, p. ix; see also Cremin 1988, p. x). That fitted the expansive organisation of Teachers College, of which he was President from 1974 to 1984, but it did not mesh with the emerging public concerns about the quality of American schooling.

Meanwhile, at other comparably distinguished research universities, the schools of education concentrated their instructional efforts on Master of Arts in Teaching programmes. Among the leaders were Chicago, Harvard, Johns Hopkins, Stanford, and Yale. Harvard, for example, in the 1950s and 1960s, nurtured and supported a broad network of colleges and universities (all private except for two), supplying potential teachers. These institutions were ones of highly selective admissions standards, thus assuring that the graduates were well-prepared academically, a rarity among US teachers nation wide. Furthermore, most of the schools in which they did their 'practice teaching' were demographically similar to many of the aspiring teachers, namely middle and upper middle class neighbourhoods where families expected their offspring to attend college, preferably prestigious ones. Harvard, for example, had a long-standing relationship with the public schools of Newton, Massachusetts, home to many professionals who sought academic excellence for their children. Harvard was happy to oblige.

Foundations and the federal government supported these initiatives in the post-Sputnik era. The Ford Foundation engaged then Harvard professor of psychology Jerome Bruner to organise a summer seminar at Woods Hole in 1959, focusing on the content of the school curriculum. Of the 31 participants only three had direct experience with schools other than as a student or parent. The remainder were successful academics who presumably lived in comfortable communities where their and their neighbours' children attended schools that prepared them for college. On this foundation rested Bruner's influential and provocative book, *The Process of Education* (1960). Undoubtedly everyone participating had experience with some youngsters who did not do well in school, but few if any understood the hidden assets that such children as their own or themselves as youngsters brought to academic study. Either they assumed that their experiences were universal or the only ones that were important in providing America with the skilled adults it needed to beat the Russians and sustain the economy.

The educators who had not been invited to the Woods Hole conference understood that the new leadership in education must address the academic needs of the 'gifted'. These were the terms of choice for those children deemed suitable for the more challenging curriculum being devised by university professors in the disciplines and often supported by the National Science Foundation, which spent more than $1.5 billion on education projects between 1954 and 1975. As Jerrold Zacharias, the MIT physicist who led the Physical Sciences Study Committee (PSSC), explained, 'We had to establish a first-class collection of stuff for the intellectual élite of the country' (Rudolph, 2002, p. 136).

In addition to Teachers College, Columbia, which was the pre-eminent school of education in the United States and indeed in the world from the early 20th century through the Second World War, two other private universities, Harvard and Stanford, have been consistent leaders in the second half of the 20th century. Chicago was also part of that group until it demoted its school of education to departmental status and then eliminated the department altogether in 1997, arguing that it had ended its involvement with teacher training and with schools and was devoting itself to theory, which evidently did not pass muster with the other Chicago faculty. During the last 50 years several public institutions, particularly the University of California both at Lost Angeles and Berkeley, the University of Michigan and the University of Wisconsin, have regularly been among the top schools of education. But all have had their troubles. Berkeley was threatened with extinction in the eighties, and Michigan was similarly threatened then and subsequently substantially reduced in size. Both Harvard and Stanford encountered severe criticism and potential demise (Harvard) or possible reduction to departmental status within the arts and sciences faculty (Stanford). These were all contemporary concerns when Judge was writing his book.

A review of the course offerings and statements of purpose of three institutions, Stanford, Harvard and Wisconsin, reveals the profound shifts in emphasis over the last 50 years. Stanford, for example, in 1958–1959, a year after Sputnik, focused its offerings on preparation of teachers and administrators, offering them various 'foundation' courses (social foundations, psychological foundations, health foundations) as well as 'educational leadership' and various curriculum and instruction sequences in school subjects. Nearly 40% (of more than 200 courses) dealt with physical education or health education. A decade later these courses were much less prominent. Schooling issues remained important, while psychological studies and testing assumed greater significance.

By 1976–1977, when Judge began work on his book, the Stanford faculty had established the disciplinary and research emphasis that transformed the curriculum with doctoral programmes in socio-humanistic studies, psychological studies, political and economic studies, mathematical methods in educational research, as well as international development education, curriculum and teacher education, and administration and policy analysis. Teacher education courses had shrunk to a minimum, mostly taught by non-tenured faculty and 'staff' who did not remain permanently at Stanford. Physical education had disappeared as a programme. The new tenured faculty included many prepared in academic disciplines, and they offered such course as 'the social sciences and educational analysis' or 'philosophy and social theory', plus various courses of their discipline applied to the study of education (history of education, sociology of education, economics of education, etc.). The 'foundations' courses, which typically were multi-disciplinary approaches to the study of education, had largely been supplanted by these.

The pattern at Harvard was similar but even more dramatic since teacher education resulting in the prestigious Master of Arts in Teaching had been a hallmark of the Harvard programme in the 1950s and 1960s. It was abolished by the School of Education senior faculty in 1974 as was the well known Administrative Career Program, which placed many prominent school superintendents in the 1950s and 1960s. Already in 1957, however, Dean Francis Keppel, a protégé of President James Bryant Conant who had selected him at the age of 31 to become dean without any advanced educational study, had begun hiring leading or extremely promising scholars in academic disciplines as faculty members at the School of Education. Among his best known recruits were historian Bernard Bailyn, philosopher Israel Scheffler, anthropologist John Whiting and literary theorist I. A. Richards. They became colleagues of such distinguished practitioners as Herold Hunt, former superintendent of schools in Chicago, who was the mainstay of the administrative training and placement programme.

By 1967 the Harvard Graduate School of Education defined its mission:

> Education is a broad and boundless subject touching all aspects of life. The domain of a graduate school of education is therefore less confined and more difficult to specify with simplicity and precision than that of almost any other professional school. Education has no restricted subject matters, is practiced by no single, unified professional group and cannot be cultivated in isolation. (Harvard University, 1967–68, p. 5)

This statement meshed well with Cremin's definition of education, but such a definition provided little guidance about what the school should emphasise. Subsequent sections focused upon academic disciplines, basic research, applied research, education of practitioners, and finally in a prescient section on 'Education and Social Problems' declared, 'the problems of poverty and racial isolation in American cities have produced a variety of efforts to find ways to integrate urban schools and improve the quality of life for the poor' (Harvard University, 1967–68, p. 10). It would take some time before the school managed to devote major attention to this matter.

A decade later in 1977–78 with its teacher and administrative education programmes abolished, Harvard defined itself differently:

> The School has expanded its focus from schooling to learning; from the conventional age-groups (elementary and secondary pupils) to learning at every age; from schools to all varieties of learning environments; from traditional curricula, delivery systems, and skills to

> contemporary versions (television as well as the classroom; interpersonal skills as wells as reading); from more narrow issues within the profession to broader questions of social goals and public policy; from the training of specialists in various aspects of schooling to the development of versatile and entrepreneurial educators. (Harvard University, 1977–78, p. 5)

Indeed, the bewildered Harvard president, Derek Bok, wondered what the school actually did and suspended tenure appointments to the school in 1975.

The University of Wisconsin, Madison, has consistently ranked among the top ten schools of education. US News and World Report, which began rankings relatively recently (1994), typically placed Harvard, Stanford and Teachers College in the top tier and Wisconsin between fifth and ninth. While rankings have many critics, most would agree that all four were leading schools of education in the last 50 years. Wisconsin, however, was a public land grant university which traditionally had placed great importance on 'serving the state'. Thus, unlike Harvard and Stanford, undergraduate teacher education assumed major significance in Madison. Its 'General Information' section of its catalogue in its 1957–58 focused entirely upon its teacher education programmes and their opportunities for student teaching at its own high school as well as 'off-campus' schools, largely populated by white middle-class children, many of whose parents were affiliated with the university, a group likely to include many 'gifted' students. Three credit courses in 'the gifted child' as well as 'education for self-adjustment' were among the offerings for juniors and seniors as well as graduate students. Courses limited to graduate students constituted less than a fourth of all the offerings. Its advanced courses were grouped into 'Education Foundations', which included Human Development, Behaviour, and Learning; Educational Survey, Theory and Criticism; and Measurement, Statistics, and Research Procedures; and 'Educational Functions', which included Administration and Supervision; Curriculum Planning and Teaching of School Subjects; Educational Diagnosis and Remediation; and Guidance and Personnel Services. In short, Wisconsin in 1957 was school-oriented and in a university known nationally for its fine research tradition, investigation of educational questions was still largely shaped by the interests of pre-war educators, not yet touched by the greater rigor of the disciplines or research design.

By 1977 teacher education still dominated and included graduate students seeking a master's degree and teacher certification with strong academic content similar to the Masters of Arts in Teaching. Research offerings became much more prominent, and educational policy studies had emerged as an area of focus with nearly two dozen 'School and Society' courses, some of which were clearly disciplinary (sociology of education) and others more comparable to their Teachers College ancestor (social issues and education).

Research university Graduate Schools of Education: 1983 to 2008

By the late 1970s Wisconsin, like Harvard and Stanford and the other leading schools of education Judge studied, was on the brink of major change, though such changes are much easier to see in retrospect than in prospect. Judge, however, recognised what he termed the 'puzzle'. The Brown decision and the Elementary and Secondary Education Act began to seep into the consciousness of the schools of education. Demands by the government to desegregate schools racially and to teach concentrations of low income children flummoxed most white, middle-class school teachers and administrators, who knew little about either. School of Education faculty members in élite universities probably knew even less since by the late 1970s relatively few senior professors (most of whom were white men) in these schools of education had taught school themselves, a contrast to an earlier generation of comparable faculty. Thus, the emphasis shifted from faculty with strong disciplinary preparation to those who could do 'policy'. The intellectual skills needed for policy were easier to acquire than ones for 'practice', about which these faculty knew relatively little. Improving educational practice for the poor and minority students was a task that few could or would tackle immediately whereas 'policy', telling others what they should do, seemed more in line with their talents and experience.

Bad news about the quality of American schools exploded again in the late 1970s and early 1980s. This time the concern was not for the 'gifted and talented', who seemed to be doing reasonably well in their special programmes and Advanced Placement classes. Universities, such as Harvard and Stanford, with demanding admissions requirements regularly called each entering class better prepared than the preceding one. Now the issue was the quality of academic preparation of the middle and lower third of the academic distribution, and those results were worrisome indeed. Willard Wirtz and his colleagues explained in 1977 the decline in Scholastic Aptitude Test performance, attributing half to new, less prepared test takers and the other half to diminished adolescent interest in schooling.

What Judge could not know in 1982, but is evident 25 years later, is that his investigation of these institutions occurred at a major turning point in Americans' attitudes toward their schools. More importantly for this study, the institutions that presumably have special responsibility for school improvement, schools of education, soon would be expected by their universities, by the public and even by some of their own faculty, administrators, students and alumni to reorient themselves. Successful schooling of the academically weak, a subject rarely encountered in these institutions in the past, emerged as a central issue for the entire society. Often the need was expressed as concern for the quality of the nation's work force, which needed to be competent to sustain the expansion of the US economy. Traditionally schools had assumed a 'take it or leave it' approach to children's academic achievement. A few were expected to do well, many would just get along, and some would fail. Vocational education was the typical solution for students uninterested in or unable to master an academic curriculum. Statisticians' bell curves describe this phenomenon. Now the terms of engagement were changing dramatically so that the bell curve no longer could justify poor academic performance. Everyone must succeed. What contribution could schools of education make to that challenge in 1982? Most were unprepared.

Ten months after Judge's volume appeared in 1982, a small blue pamphlet issued by a commission appointed by the US Secretary of Education most improbably caught the attention of the American public and subsequently the American federal government. This document, entitled *A Nation at Risk*, dramatically asserted that the US was endangered because its children were not receiving schooling appropriate for their effective participation in the workforce and in the democracy. Mastery of dramatic infusions of academic material was sought for all. This demand was radical in ways no other 'reform' had ever been, challenging not simply the financing, governance, or organisation of schooling but rather its consequences. While this report caught the national fancy, to the amazement of its authors, it was only one of a half a dozen reports and books that appeared at that time echoing essentially the same theme. In short, significant numbers of Americans were concerned about the educational achievement of the entire nation's youth.

Unlike previous critiques of American schooling, this one stimulated federal action, most improbably from Republican administrations, which had previously favoured a very limited role for the federal government in public schooling. In fact, President Ronald Reagan's Secretary of Education, Terrel Bell, had commissioned *A Nation at Risk* in an effort to stave off Republicans' elimination of the new federal Department of Education. Nonetheless, 20 years later Republican President George W. Bush led and the US Congress enacted in 2002, with rare bi-partisan support, 'No Child Left Behind' legislation. It mandated academic tests for maintenance of federal funds with a variety of other unpleasant consequences flowing if scores were not universally high. The result for many children, particularly those from low income families, was indeed to leave both them and their schools behind when they failed the tests as many did. School administrators and teachers have scrambled to meet this new requirement.

These circumstances bring us to the current issues for American schools of education in research universities. Should they turn their attention exclusively to this task of helping beleaguered teachers and administrators find ways that will allow their schools to meet the required goals of 'Annual Yearly Progress'? Are there broader issues that these schools of education should consider? If so, what are they? How is the balance to be struck among competing priorities for schools of education?

The recent history of these schools of education, like their past, is turbulent. Gone is the conviction that the only good research is that which is accepted by the relevant academic department; gone is the primary and preferred focus upon preparing teachers for affluent and 'gifted' children. Gone is the widespread development of rich curriculum materials intended to excite a child intellectually. While policy discussions still occur, most are supplemented now by discussions of practice. Major research attention has shifted from the discipline-based studies to practice-based quantitative research. Methodologically sophisticated research designs dominate, occasionally obscuring important aspects of the issue under investigation, which do not fit the design metrics. For example, much work exists on per-pupil expenditure in schools, loosely described to reveal the costs of 'education', but most do not account for family and community resources invested in the child's actual education.

Most important of all, the child whose educational needs now compel attention is not the one who does well in school, but rather the one whose performance as measured by state-mandated tests is not satisfactory. Faculty, administrators and students at these schools of education all recognise a central conundrum: we know that public schools exist which serve low income, minority children well and in which these students score on tests above—often well above—similarly-situated children and appear to be enthusiastic about their school. What we do not know is how to replicate broadly the qualities of the school that are central to students' academic performance and enthusiasm.

What is also striking about these schools of education at present is how attentive they are to issues of schooling, which nearly disappeared from their attention in earlier decades. The pendulum has swung furthest at Harvard. In 1983 nearly the identical senior faculty of the school of education which had eliminated teacher education courses a decade earlier voted to resume them, initially with a mid-career mathematics and science teacher programme, followed closely by a resumption of a master's programme for beginning teachers, and then with a programme for undergraduates at Harvard to complete both their BA degree and teacher certification simultaneously. During the same decade Harvard reinstituted administrative training for principals and then created the Urban Superintendents Program, which focused entirely upon persons intending to work in schools serving low income families. In short, the shift from the rich to the poor, from non-school educational issues to schools, from disciplinary research to inquiries into improving practice was underway. The presidents of the university (Bok and Neil Rudenstine) supported this transition, granting tenure to all the candidates proposed by the school of education faculty, a rarity in Harvard administrative practice. By 2006 a collaborative effort of School of Education faculty and staff had developed a web site, 'Usable Knowledge: Connecting Research and Practice'. The School of Education now embraced the notion of the utility of knowledge, central to most professional schools, but at considerable contrast to earlier statements of purpose.

Stanford and Wisconsin made similar shifts in their activities. Stanford reinforced its commitment to schooling initially through senior appointments of experts in teaching and school administration, such as Lee Shulman, Larry Cuban and Linda Darling-Hammond. They joined a powerful research faculty, some of whom shared their interests in schooling and others whose primary commitment was to educational research more broadly defined, often with a strong disciplinary component. In 1986–87 Stanford described itself as 'responsible for the preparation of scholars investigating educational processes, and of teachers, supervisors, guidance workers, administrators, and other educational specialists' (*Stanford University Bulletin*, 1986–87, p. 59). A decade later, 'scholars' still led the list, which now included 'teachers, teacher educators, counselling psychologists, policy analysts, evaluators, researchers, administrators and other educational specialists' (*Stanford University Bulletin*, 1996–97, p. 106). Presently Stanford maintains the same commitment except for 'counselling psychologists', who have been dropped from the list. Its current courses abound with analyses and investigations of the learning needs of children who have often had difficulty in school ('education of immigrant students', 'teaching and learning in heterogeneous classrooms') while maintaining a strong group of theoretical, methodological and disciplinary based offerings ('social justice and education', 'application of hierarchical linear models in behavioural and social research', 'human cognitive abilities'). Stanford has also recently undertaken to operate schools in its low income neighbouring community of East Palo Alto, California, an effort in sharp contrast to the tradition of schools of education working with the children of the privileged in their 'lab' schools or professional development schools. Stanford's success in this venture is not yet assured.

The Wisconsin tradition of preparing school teachers was deeply ingrained, but by 1986 its mission statement began:

> The School of Education is a professional school with primary emphasis upon the preparation of personnel for educational systems ... The school provides instruction for undergraduates and graduates in educational professions, facilitates the development of scholarship and research on the nature of learners, learning environments, and the learning process at all ages and in all contexts; and furnishes inservice programs for a broadly based educational community. (University of Wisconsin, Madison, 1968–88, p. 3)

This more expansive and bureaucratic definition reflected the tension between school-based activities, long a staple of the Wisconsin education programme, and broader research investigations. The School of Education at Wisconsin is much larger than those at either Harvard or Stanford, and its division into such departments as Curriculum and Instruction and Educational Administration, now called Educational Leadership and Policy Analysis, reflected its long involvement with schools. Other departments, particularly Educational Psychology and Educational Policy Studies, are home to the faculty with strong disciplinary interests. In addition, unlike Harvard or Stanford, Wisconsin's School of Education maintains separate departments of Kinesiology, Rehabilitation Psychology and Special Education, and Counselling Psychology. These latter programmes broaden the spectrum of the school's interests considerably and are typical of many universities.

The Wisconsin Center for Education Research (WCER), which operates jointly with faculty both from the school of education and from other departments in the university, such as political science or sociology, provides a focus on educational questions on the Madison campus. Founded in 1964 just as federal funding for educational research became available, WCER now employs 350 faculty, staff and students on 60 projects with an annual budget of approximately $25 million. Financial support has come largely from the federal government and from foundations; thus, its priorities have changed accordingly. Nonetheless, it has been a leader in the educational research community. In addition, a number of other multi-disciplinary research institutes on the Madison campus investigated subjects related to education, particularly the Institute for Research on Poverty.

Slowly, always more slowly than the public would like, these schools of education are attempting to understand and to remedy the problems of practice that make learning for some students so hard. The faculty of these schools of education share with the students they now study a common bond: they too have difficulty in learning. The academics' dilemma is how to universalise schools with rich intellectual content and supports for all children to master it. In short, how to increase children's 'wit'. But also, schools are still expected to nurture children's character, traditionally considered more important than their wit, by fostering ingenuity, integrity, responsibility, respect and capacity to work alone and with others. Moreover, in America and most other countries, schools also have a responsibility for moulding the citizenry. Judge's schools of education build on their old accomplishments, such as infusing educational research with disciplinary rigour, while attempting to address the current dilemmas. These enormous demands challenge all their capacities, but they should not suffer concern that their work is unimportant, only difficult. Undoubtedly, the report in a quarter century from now will again speculate on past accomplishments, failures and current needs.

Acknowledgements

The author, while assuming full responsibility for this article, is indebted to several colleagues who have read or commented upon it: pre-eminently research librarian at Harvard Graduate School of Education, Patrice Moskow, and William Baldwin, Elisabeth Hansot, Susan Fuhrman, Michael Fultz, Kathleeen McCartney, Katherine Merseth, Richard Murnane, Jerry Murphy, David Null, Arthur Powell, John Rudolph, Theodore Sizer and David Tyack.

References

Bestor, A. (1953) *Educational Wastelands: The Retreat from Learning in our Public Schools* (Urbana, University of Illinois Press).

Bestor, A. (1955) *The Restoration of Learning: A Program for Redeeming the Unfulfilled Promise of American Education* (New York, Alfred A. Knopf).

Bruner, J. (1960) *The process of education* (Cambridge, MA, Harvard University Press).

Cremin, L. A. (1980) *American Education: The National Experience: 1783-1876* (New York, Harper & Row).

Cremin, L. A. (1988) *American Education: The Metropolitan Experience: 1876-1980* (New York, Harper & Row).

Flesch, R. (1955) *Why Johnny Can't Read* (New York, John Wiley).

Harvard University (1967-68) *Harvard Graduate School of Education Catalogue 1967-68* (Cambridge, MA, Harvard University).

Harvard University (1977-78) *Harvard Graduate School of Education Catalogue 1977-78* (Cambridge, MA, Harvard University).

Judge, Harry (1982) *American Graduate Schools of Education: a view from abroad* (New York, The Ford Foundation).
Rickover, H. (1962) *Swiss Schools and Ours: Why theirs are Better* (Boston, Little Brown).
Rudolph, J. (2002) *Scientists in the Classroom* (New York, Palgrave).
Stanford University Bulletin, 1986–87, Stanford, CA.
Stanford University Bulletin, 1996–97, Stanford, CA.
University of Wisconsin, Madison (1986-88) *Bulletin of School of Education 1986-88* (University of Wisconsin, Madison).

The University and the Teachers: a cross-national experience

Michel Lemosse
University of Nice, France

The totally unusual experience of participating in the writing of *The University and the Teachers: France, the United States, England* is recalled here by one of the co-authors. This was a collective enterprise, under the direction of Harry Judge, and the other members of the team were two American researchers, Lynn Paine and Michael Sedlak. The book was conceived as a cross-national comparison, and the authors agreed to exercise their 'expert ignorance'. This writer was, as a result, invited to observe and interpret the American situtation, while Harry Judge wrote the chapters on France.

The comparative method devised by Harry Judge and used for the elaboration and the writing of the collective book *The University and the Teachers*, published in 1994 by Triangle Books, deserves close examination. It was applied to the study of teacher education, and more specifically the scope and the mode of the involvement of universities in teacher training, in three countries: France, England and the United States.

It may very well be that, had I been asked to play Harry Judge's role, I would have proceeded along traditional lines. I would have been happy, presumably, to call on three local experts and invite them to describe and analyse their own national teacher education systems in three parallel chapters, to which would have been added some sort of synthetic conclusion in order to collect the main strands and threads. Who else but the national experts could have earnestly been trusted to perform the task? Who else possessed a better knowledge of the historical sources, their understanding and interpretation? Who else was able to make sense of it all?

Harry Judge himself was one of the best equipped scholars in his own country to write on teacher education in England at least on two accounts: he had himself been at the helm in the Department of Educational Studies at Oxford, and had produced excellent books and articles on the subject. With him, theory and practice were ideally blended. His involvement with Michigan State University (among others in the United States), on the other hand, was a guarantee that he would very easily find the best American candidate among existing historians of education. As for the chapter on France, a country which he knew so well as an historian and researcher, he had already met most (if not all) of the French academics who were qualified to write on the development of teacher education in the nation, under the monarchy and then the republic.

Why he would not follow this solid yet conventional, rigorous though limited method, was not clear to me immediately. And I was left to wonder at the beginning why I had been invited to be part of the team at all. As a French scholar whose main field of research was the history of education in England (and Wales), what role could I be expected to fulfil? In my own (narrow) view, I was not qualified to write about France. My own experience might have been of historical interest: I had gone into teacher training in a 'normal school' to be a primary school teacher; this had been followed by college education at the Sorbonne where I obtained a degree and the proud title of *professeur agrégé*; and subsequently I had embarked upon an academic career. Obviously, I had some insights into teacher education in my own country, as well as some views of its strengths and weaknesses. But this could not reasonably pass for genuine scholarship. Would I be asked then to contribute to the chapter on England? There were dozens of English colleagues who would perform the task with a higher level of expertise.

Harry Judge saw things differently. He trusted insiders, of course, and was professionally well aware of the quality and quantity of national scholarship which could be mustered to serve his comparative as well as contrastive enterprise. But this time he was determined to call upon outsiders in order to obtain a set of different, fresher perspectives on the core subject: the history of the involvement of universities in teacher education in three Western democracies so close to one another and at the same time culturally and politically so remote. Instead of parallel studies conducted from within, what he sought to obtain was a cross-national perspective. The original, innovative approach therefore consisted in inviting foreigners to look at the historical evolution of teacher training in three different countries and observe how it came willy-nilly to be absorbed into the world of universities. The underlying assumption was that while the insider might take too much for granted and fail to see what is only too familiar to him, the outsider by nature was inclined to look at alien customs, traditions and innovations with a mixture of surprise and occasionally disbelief. His motivation to understand and account for what he observes is therefore heightened.

As an outsider, Harry Judge had already explored the field of American teacher education. In 1982, for the Ford Foundation, he had published *American Graduate Schools of Education: a view from abroad*. This book will long remain a model, I am sure, for writers who wish to take a distanced, balanced view of a foreign scene and at the same time make sure that their representation never betrays their object. Harry was amply qualified to write the chapters on the United States. He preferred instead to concentrate on France, probably because there remained more to find out for him across the Channel than over the Atlantic. His status as an outsider would be more authentic.

The work on England was entrusted not to one, but two, American scholars. I was never able to figure out why exactly two excellent American minds were needed to survey the English scene when one apparently was enough for the United States or France. Could it be that, by nature, English history and society engendered a more elaborate form of complexity compared to the others, of a rougher, coarser kind? Both were selected from Michigan State University. Lynn Paine had carried out research as an insider on teacher education policy and practice, teacher education and teaching, educational reform and social change. But she was also an experienced outsider, having conducted much of her research in China and participated in a cross-national study of a comparative nature. Michael Sedlak added the expertise of the historian, with an eye more specifically trained to the American scene: by the time he joined the team, he was known for his interpretive history of education in the United States (1976), and his book on *Classrooms, bargains and academic reform in the American High School*, which charged the education system with selling students short (1986).

I was left with the immense task of making sense of the past trends and present state of the relationship between teacher education and American universities, a journey taking me from the narrow confines of a geographically small nation, whether it be Britain or France, to the vast expanses of a whole continent. And what a journey it was, to a seemingly boundless land where none of the things which I had taken for granted in my preparation for and exercise of my profession appeared to be taken seriously. Not that I had never been abroad before. I had taught in anglophone and francophone Africa. The main body of my academic research and publications was on the history of education in England and Wales. My Doctorat d'Etat had been centered on teacher unions in Britain, quite an unsettling adventure if one thinks of the contrasts with their counterparts in France: here too your inbred assumptions had to be cast away if you earnestly wished to understand the issues of structure, behaviour and strategies.

What we all shared was a common qualification, as Harry Judge put it, in 'expert ignorance', a fine oxymoron which proved to be a source of bliss as well as of woe in the process of our work. The pleasure which arose from the sensation of being knowledgeable academics in a foreign land was for ever vying with the pain that came with the awareness of our own ignorance. But this was precisely, and paradoxically perhaps, Harry's aim. Not that he particularly wanted us to suffer. But he saw there the necessary condition for the sharpening of our observers' minds. By expert ignorance, he wished to insist that (i) we would be exploring a field of study which would be in itself familiar to us but (ii) in a national context where almost everything observed would strike us as being somewhat strange or unsettling. We would become discoverers. This was the case for each of us: Harry had yet to figure out what kind of institutions the French *écoles normales* for the training of primary school teachers had been, and how the new colleges of education or *instituts universitaires de formation des maîtres*, which were being set up in each *académie*, had been conceived or what was expected of them. Michael and Lynn had never set foot in Britain and teacher training in the sceptered isle was to them at the beginning shrouded in mystery. In my own case, my experience of the United States was limited to New England, and I had never seen an American campus, or been anywhere near a School of Education before.

This state of relative innocence can be frightening. Here before you lies this *terra incognita*. How on earth will you blaze your own trail, and make some sense of what is going on there after only a limited number of visits? The volume of knowledge to be stored, sifted and assimilated seems at first truly dissuasive and forbidding. It is hard then not to think that the whole undertaking is overambitious. And yet the initial condition of ignorance offers a major advantage which justifies the method used. It guarantees that your distanced, relatively naïve observation and assessment of the scene steer clear of the pitfalls inherent in self-examination. A self-portrait may be in turns complacent, narcissistic or unduly critical. Very rarely will it be neutral, objective and detached. Whether I like it or not, my ability to give a dispassionate account of my own education system will be impaired by my own prejudices or preferences as well as by the identity of my addressee.

Let me quote just two examples taken from my own national context: the existence of competitive examinations organised on a national basis to select secondary school teachers on the one hand, and the status of teachers as civil servants (i.e. employed, appointed, paid and inspected by the State) on the other. Now there is an overall, almost universal consensus in France that these are two of the main cornerstones of the education system. Remove one, and the whole structure is sure to collapse. There have been at times suggestions that the selection of teachers might be made on a local basis by school heads, for example. In this case, the competitive examinations (the *Capes* and, at a higher level, the *agrégation*) would simply have to go. Such proposals have repeatedly been drowned under howls of protest from the profession, which tends to see in the meritocratic tradition of such *concours* the best guarantee that would-be teachers are assessed on no other basis than their academic grasp of their subjects first of all, and then their ability to teach them. Likewise, their status as civil servants instead of local employees is regarded as the safest protection of their professional autonomy (in his/her own class, the teacher, appointed by the Ministry of Education and not by the school, does not have to answer to the head on the nature of his/her teaching). In a comparative and contrastive study of the kind which Harry Judge devised, such sacred truths are bound of course to be put under the microscope or dissected without any particular qualms. An unprejudiced outsider may find that the dependence on an all-powerful state may not after all produce all the freedom that is claimed, or that a little more local control might bring the schools closer to the communities which they serve. In other words, under the glaring light of research conducted from outside, basic premises always run the risk of looking like old shibboleths. This is one of the things that I have learned from working alongside my American and English colleagues. Some of my own beliefs were at times badly shaken. My faith did not dissolve in the process, but it was undoubtedly transformed.

Another problem which emerged at the time, not of the observation and investigation of the field of study, but of the actual process of writing, was that of the identification of your potential reader. That you should have this reader next to you, always within easy reach, so to speak, when you are writing, goes without saying. Even the most abstract form of writing cannot be very far from story-telling, in the sense that it remains basically an act of communication. What the four of us had to say on our research findings involved identifying a reader and passing on to him/her what knowledge we thought we had acquired in a manner which, ideally, made complex realities not simpler, but clear and intelligible in his/her own cultural environment. In a cross-national enterprise of the sort which we had launched into, this was obviously easier said than done. It was difficult enough for my American and English friends. But at least they were addressing an English-speaking readership. Even if common assumptions can greatly differ on either side of the Atlantic, much is shared on the level of educational concepts and terminology. Writers and readers were bound by the same language and a familiar mode of discourse.

In my own case, I was naturally inclined to assume that my potential reader, whom I was supposed to introduce to the characteristics and peculiarities of American teacher education in its university context, was someone close enough to me, with a broad interest in the history of education, pretty little knowledge at first of the subject, and similar preconceptions or expectations. We would also speak the same language. This was a major mistake, of course. The book was to be published in England and written in English. Statistically, the proportion of French readers would be minimal. I was going in fact to write for American colleagues who might not be pleased at all with my historical presentation of their professional world. My other readers would be British, eager perhaps to learn about the American experience, but slightly or seriously disoriented by my idiosyncratic approach. This double-headed creature that was to be my basic reader had somehow to be tamed and appeased by an array of stylistic and narrative precautions which were new to me and had to be invented for the occasion.

The best writers of non-fictional texts are those, in my opinion, who manage to blend, in one sentence, factual information, their own comment, in however blunt or subtle a form, and their personal voice. Facts alone are boring. Comments without the backbones of facts are vapid and pointless. And the voice, singular and distinctive, is what differentiates you from the machine. Ideally of course, good writing is the delicate fusion of all three elements. This is a stylistic feature which I have learnt from reading Harry Judge, among a few others. As a humble emulator, I have made great efforts to adopt and follow that rule. But how do you balance fact and comment when your reader assumes a dual identity, when one half of the creature wants to be told the full story from sheer ignorance, and the other would rather not for the simple reason that this is common knowledge? What, under these circumstances, is the ideal dosage? More than ten years later, I still cannot tell. But it was a stimulating challenge.

Then came the voice. If the image of the likely readers remained blurred, at least the narrator and commentator could be more easily identified. Now this is not always regarded as wise or advisable, especially in a mode of scientific discourse, where the observer should remain hidden and largely anonymous. Hence the use of a style that is as impersonal as can be, with traces of subjective sentiment carefully suppressed. I decided to do just the opposite. After all, even if he avoids the pitfalls of self-examination, any outside observer remains a human being made of flesh and blood, with his own cultural roots, estranged from the object of his study by a number of prejudices and preferences. Why not be honest with your reader and make a clean breast of this at the outset? This was how I became convinced that I ought to write one or two introductory pages of self-presentation, simply to highlight the distance between my observation post and those American campuses where teacher education of a very different character had taken root. My contribution to the book, therefore, begins on a highly personal note. Harry, I am sure, would have preferred a more discreet, less self-centred introduction, but in the end never exercised his right of veto, for which I remain extremely grateful to him. The issue is still open. What is at stake is, as in the case of historical narratives, the degree of personal commitment and subjectivity which the author is prepared to confess or exhibit.

The cross-national comparison based on the principle of 'expert ignorance' was innovative enough. We never discussed the dangers among ourselves, probably because we were so thrilled by the adventure. But if this was to some extent a trip into the unknown, we also felt the need, on Harry's recommendation, to minimise the heavy risks, tread on some safe ground, and carefully stake out our field of research. This was how one thematic element was chosen to ensure that our diverse studies would focus on the same narrow topic: the relationship of universities to teacher education. A similar thread, historical in nature, would also connect the three studies: 1963 was taken as a starting point for each of our expositions.

Just defined as a 'narrow' topic, the theme of the involvement of universities in teacher education is also, of course, of essential importance. This was clear enough when we embarked on our research, and it became even more obvious as we proceeded with our visits, interviews and investigations in the early 1990s. In England, for example, the Conservative government was pursuing the argument that teacher training would best be wrenched away from higher education institutions and entrusted to the schools themselves (which were less than keen to add to their present burden). After the creation of a centrally controlled Teacher Training Agency, 'teacher educators', wrote the American colleagues, 'seemed shell-shocked'. Their conclusion reads: 'In 1994, wrenched from its home of a century in higher education yet unwelcomed by those whom the government hoped would adopt it, teacher education in England appears to be on the verge of becoming homeless' (*The University and the Teachers*, p. 239). In France, on the other hand, the issue was of a totally different nature. The vast transformation which was going on did not consist in removing teacher training from higher education but, on the contrary, in making sure that the professional training of all prospective teachers, including those in the primary sector, would take place within higher education. 'Normal schools' which had offered such training to *instituteurs* (elementary school teachers) were condemned to disappear. The new institutions, set up in 1990–1991, were called *Instituts Universitaires de Formation des Maîtres* (IUFMs), and there was much speculation as to what would come under the *U* for *Universitaire*. I witnessed no such dramatic changes in the United States. Any sharp distinction between elementary and high school teachers had long been lost and would have indeed seemed an aberration. Professional training in higher education was likewise a long tradition. But this did not mean that teacher educators were always feeling comfortable in their academic environment. As John Goodlad remarked in 1990, teaching seemed condemned to remain the 'not-quite profession'. The preparation of teachers was rarely seen to rank as high as that of lawyers and doctors. Or, as it soon became clear to me, writing as a scholar on the history of education still carried much more prestige than training teachers.

Finally, there arose the basic question of the use of history to explain the present scene of teacher education within its university context, in the three countries, and in the early 1990s. One solution, as Harry Judge put it, was to write history 'forwards', that is to cover the full length of the 20th century until its last decade and hope, against all odds, to make it intelligible. An alternative method was adopted which was just as innovative as the reliance on the principle of 'expert ignorance'. A pivotal year, 1963, was taken to be appropriate as a starting point for all three countries. Each of the three studies begins with an overview of the situation in that year. Then we were asked, in Harry's words, to write 'outwards, from the middle'. This provided a unifying framework for the cross-national stories, with a common focus on the mid-sixties, followed by a retrospective view and then an analysis of the thirty years that followed.

The conclusion which Harry Judge contributed to the book took us all by surprise, but still rings as true as it did then, more than a decade ago. The French observer, he wrote, saw the United States as a 'jungle'— 'luxuriant, confusing, noisy, undisciplined, competitive, diverse, unmanaged, individualistic, unsystematic'. The American colleagues, on the other hand, viewed England 'perhaps more like a zoo: caged, fragmented, tidy, domesticated, deferential, inflexible, generally docile'. For his own part, he himself was more inclined to admire France 'as a circus: planned, orchestrated, elegant, geometric, traditional, skilful, moving at the behest of an always invisible ringmaster' (*The University and the Teachers*, p. 262). Jungle, zoo or circus, the ignorant experts that we were had indeed been called upon to visit uncanny places, which we had sought to depict as accurately as we could with the sharpness of our foreign gaze. The three metaphors aptly conveyed the notions of diversity as well as otherness and exoticness, and at the same time suggested that our experiences had not been fundamentally different.

Ultimately, though, this 'jungle, zoo or circus' encapsulation of the book led Harry to reflect that while we were concentrating on IUFMs, schools, colleges or departments of education, universities and teachers, prior to or since 1963, we were also observing the societies in which they were all embedded. Hence the final paradox: 'perhaps after all it would have been wiser to choose another subject', like contrasting British Rail with SNCF and Amtrak. With none of the trappings of an expert, and the full awareness of my abysmal ignorance in this subject, I would nonetheless be extremely happy to start afresh, provided Harry cheered us on again.

Knowledge and teaching

David K. Cohen
University of Michigan, USA

This paper concerns a puzzle about teachers' knowledge. That special knowledge of academic subjects is an essential asset in teachers' work, for the more they know the greater their resources for helping learners. Yet that knowledge also is a liability, for the more accomplished teachers are in a field, the more finished their knowledge is. That finished material properly represents teachers' intellectual accomplishments, but it typically is quite remote from learners' tentative and often puzzling formulations. How can teachers use such knowledge to help learners who are only beginners?

Introduction

I began work on the ideas in this contribution at about the time that I first met Harry Judge. He was visiting the US to do the research for his book on graduate schools of education, and I was teaching at Harvard's Graduate School of Education. My conversation with him then was fascinating and refreshing. One reason was that, unlike so many of my colleagues, he understood that the education of teachers was, or should be, the central activity of such professional schools. The other reason was that when we met I had recently begun work on a related puzzle, namely, to understand what sort of a practice was teaching?

I came to that question on a different path than Harry had come to his work on teaching. I had been studying education policies for several decades, and remarking, mostly to myself, that they often made apparently implausible assumptions about the teaching that they sought to change. I finally decided that, rather than just remarking that and moving on, I would investigate it. What sort of work did teachers do, and how, what resources did they require, how did teaching compare with other practices, and, finally, how might it best be influenced by those who sought to improve it?

Harry's trip and his book helped to begin a period of increasing scholarly attention to teaching and teacher education in the US, and, for better and worse, increasing attention from politicians. Harry was a significant influence on the first development, as I believe Ed Meade, the educator and Ford Foundation official who sponsored Harry's investigation, had hoped his work would be. It also began more than a decade of my colleagueship with Harry, some of it attached to wine, and some to curiously amusing signs that we collected together. But most of our conversations attached to teaching and teacher education. Though I do not think that I ever inflicted drafts of my project on Harry, they profited from our many conversations about teaching and teacher education. It is fitting that Harry Judge, whose academic work had been in history, should have helped to make a bit of history in the field into which he found his way from the study of the past.

Learning is an ordinary human endeavour. Anyone reading this page has learned many thousands of things, quite likely including how to dress themselves, how to speak a language, how to drive a car, and how to cook a meal. Some have learned more unusual things, like how to read a foreign language or do algebra. Presumably everyone has learned how to make some sense out of sentences like these. But if such learning is utterly commonplace it also is quite remarkable, for no-one can learn unless they try to do things that they do not know how to do. I could not have learned to swim unless I got into the water and tried to swim, even though I did not know how to. Unless I tried and failed I could not begin to swim, nor could I hope to grasp what remained to be learned. But I could not swim. There was no help for it. I had to get into the water and thrash, choke, sink, look silly, wish I were somewhere else, and intermittently rue the day I decided to learn to swim. There is no other way to learn swimming than to try it, and I was not one of those rare birds to whom swimming came easily.

Learning is paradoxical: we can learn only by sailing the boats that we are trying to build. We cannot really sail them because they are not yet built, but we can only build these boats by trying to sail them. This is a terrific puzzle, and sometimes a terrifying one. Many readers will recall the blank they drew when first trying to swim, or drive, or work an addition problem. Some also will remember the ensuing worry, or even panic. Yet humans all over the earth learn, millions of times every day.

Teachers face a different problem. They sail more finished boats, and have found at least a few courses on which to manoeuvre. But their professional assignment is to help others who are less accomplished. They must reach out from craft already built and cruising a familiar course, to learners whose boats are only begun, who are moving tentatively, or on a puzzling course, or seem dead in the water.

They do so in part by extending knowledge to learners. They lecture, write, make homework assignments, compose computer courses and in many other ways launch knowledge toward learners. Teachers' knowledge is an essential asset in such work, for the more they know the greater their resources for helping learners. Yet equally learned teachers extend knowledge in very different ways. Some try to unpack knowledge in order to render it accessible. They use metaphors, analogies, and other intellectual inventions, as well as drawing pictures, making diagrams, and using apparatus in efforts to present and re-present ideas to learners. Teachers who work in such ways try to extend knowledge so that it will be open to learners—that is, they will be able to find varied routes into it, and paths through it, thus increasing the connections learners may make.[1]

But if teachers' knowledge is an essential asset in their work, it also is a liability. For the more accomplished teachers are in a field, the more finished their knowledge is. They find it convenient and even elegant to extend knowledge in polished and highly compressed form. Such finished material often nicely represents teachers' intellectual accomplishments, but it usually is quite remote from learners' tentative and often puzzling formulations. Because they do not unpack knowledge, teachers who work in this way limit the routes by which students gain access to it and the paths they can find through it.

Consider another metaphor. Teachers and learners face the same chasms of ignorance, though from different sides. Learners must somehow build bridges across, but the structures they create often are fragile and modestly developed. It could hardly be otherwise, since they work from relative ignorance. Teachers' assignment is to help learners to build those bridges, but they work from the other side, building back from greater competence. That they do reflects an essential qualification, for ignorant teachers would be no help. Yet their competence means that most teachers see learners' bridges from the perspective of finished knowledge, an angle from which learners' constructions seem fragile, jerry-built, and incapable of supporting much traffic. Most teachers respond by extending finished bridges back and insisting that students use them whole. Instead of helping learners to construct and reconstruct bridges of their own they press the finished result of their own learning on students.[2]

That teachers do such things should be no surprise. For to learn well is to consolidate knowledge, to finish it, and once that is done, earlier formulations seem unsatisfying and clumsy. Finished work is much more elegant and pleasing, and it seems only right to convey it to learners, especially since that is what they should wind up with. The achievement of some intellectual competence, which is a necessary condition of teaching, also is a handicap in it.

Knowledge extension

Teachers everywhere extend knowledge in finished form. One familiar example can be found in mathematics instruction. Teachers from first grade to graduate school work problems as efficiently as they can. They stand at the board or overhead projector and announce that they are 'showing' students how mathematics is done as they work through a problem. Once the example is complete students are enjoined to 'practise,' i.e., to work the problem and others like it, as the teacher has. Such demonstrations present a condensed version of mathematical problem solving, and the unspoken assumption is that students need only follow the example in order to learn maths. Teaching of this sort in universities sometimes offers elegant examples of finished work, while in elementary classrooms it often consists only of a compressed and mechanised version of arithmetic.

In either case, teachers present instances of the desired end state of learning that are quite remote from the typical fumbling, fits-and-starts ways that mathematicians and students of mathematics work. Instruction in writing often is similar. Teachers read good writing aloud, or assign it to learners, or perhaps copy it on the board, then they hand out paper and invite students to write a story or essay on a similar theme. These teachers appear to assume that in order to write well one need only follow the example and practice, neglecting to mention that the writing they read was the result of many false starts and revisions.

It has long been fashionable to scoff at such teaching. John Dewey was only the most distinguished of many 19th-century commentators to deride it. Like Pestalozzi and dozens of others in Europe and the US, he argued that presenting knowledge in its finished, 'adult' form was a foolish effort to cram dead stuff into live minds. Dewey and many earlier commentators argued that knowledge should be 'psychologised'—i.e., presented so that it fitted with children's more concrete and vital modes of thought.[3] Jean Piaget gave these ideas great scientific *cachet* in his studies of children's intellectual development. The idea that knowledge should be represented in distinctive ways to accord with learners' 'stages' of intellectual development has since become a sort of orthodoxy, especially in the emphasis on 'concrete operations' in primary education.

But if it is foolish to teach by extending finished synopses toward students, it is a nearly ubiquitous and entirely reasonable foolishness. One cannot begin to grasp what it takes to construct an artful practice of teaching unless one understands why this foolishness makes such good sense. To begin, consider how we learn, or used to learn the proper use of the clutch, when beginning to drive. Teaching in this case often consists of the instructor saying something of the following sort: 'Just let the clutch out slowly, while accelerating gently'.

While this is a correct description of the operation, it offers a vastly compressed synopsis of an entire set of procedures. There is no reference to the many sub-routines that contribute to successfully '... let[ting] the clutch out slowly while accelerating gently'. The teacher has extended a fair summary of what the intending driver needs to do, but like all synoptic teaching it offers little sense of what is contained in the doing. One reason teachers find such synopses reasonable is that they seem transparently clear, as well they should. An experienced driver has so thoroughly routinised and integrated the many sub-routines contained in clutch and accelerator coordination that the synopsis accurately portrays their speedy, polished performances. The knowledge that teachers extend toward students in such cases is literally what they do, or better, are aware of doing. Hence it is not surprising that they grow impatient when students repeatedly stall the car, or profess continued incomprehension about working the clutch. Nor is it surprising that such teachers respond by simply reasserting that, '... it's perfectly clear—just let the clutch out slowly while accelerating gently'.

It is easy to say that teachers should explain more, or demonstrate, but their exasperated repetition masks a large problem. Accomplished drivers would have to work quite hard to re-discover and make explicit all the sub-routines in their smooth clutch-and-accelerator work. I say re-discover because learning to drive is in part a matter of consciously learning and then automating many such operations, thus dispatching them from conscious attention and leaving the mind free to attend to oncoming cars or passing a truck. But it is just those individual sub-routines and their coordination that each new driver must learn, and for them the teacher's compressed sentences are mysterious. That is not surprising either, since novices know nothing of the operations thus summarised and can barely perform as drivers.[4] Hence their baffled pleas to '... please explain it just once more'. Between teachers' impatiently repeated synopses and learners' pleas for more explanation there lies a great gulf, one that separates teachers and learners of many different sorts.

Novices nonetheless learn in the neighbourhood of such teaching. How do they do it? In driving they commonly put the hapless automobiles into a series of convulsive, choking, fits and starts. Like greenhorns astride maddened broncos, they don't know why the beasts are behaving so badly, or how the problem might be corrected. Teachers often are reduced to gritting their teeth, or shouting 'floor the clutch', or 'use less gas', or 'stop!'. The wear and tear on cars, people, and family ties can be appreciable. But in the end most intending drivers figure out a way to release the clutch while increasing the gas in more or less independent trials and errors with clutch, gas, and convulsions as their teachers look on, talk, cringe, shout, and worry.

If anyone doubts that this sort of teaching is synoptic, consider an alternative. A driving teacher begins by telling her student that he is going to learn how to operate the clutch. She explains that the clutch permits drivers to make or break the connection between the engine and the driving wheels, which enables drivers to start, stop, and change gears without stalling, stripping the gears, or worse. The teacher then says that this part of learning to drive will occur in several different ways. She will discuss the clutch and its operation. Then she will rehearse the steps in controlling the clutch, and after that the learner will try a few dry runs. Then he will make some small trials in a safe parking lot, and only after all that will the student actually try to drive on the street.

The teacher then pulls out a drawing of the automotive drive train and locates the clutch in it. She also displays a working model of the clutch and traces its operation. She identifies the two circular plates that are the heart of the device, shows how they are engaged and disengaged by being slipped together or pulled apart, explains that such a frictional arrangement permits gradual engagement and disengagement rather than simple on/off action, and shows how slippage helps when starting and shifting through the gears. She works the model and asks questions about its operation until the student seems to grasp the matter.

After this overview the teacher moves into a dry run. First she puts the emergency brake on, places the transmission in neutral, starts the engine, shifts into first and slowly engages the clutch. When it begins to catch she quickly depresses it to prevent a stall. She invites the student to repeat these steps verbally and traces the student's account on the working model. She then asks the student to slide into the driver's seat and practise the operations several times with the engine off. She follows his operations on the model and relates them to the model's movements.

When her student seemed to grasp these operations and their place in the car's operation, she invites him to try it with the engine on and the transmission in neutral. If that goes well she asks him to slowly but only partly release the clutch with the engine on but the emergency brake engaged, to get the feel of the clutch as it begins to engage. Then she drives to an empty lot, stops, and asks the student to start the engine, shift into first gear, and practise starting and stopping the car. Once that seemed to be under control the teacher would begin the next steps—i.e., teaching the student to shift up through the gears while driving in the lot, and then on a quiet street.

An unpacked approach of this sort would familiarise learners with the operations entailed in '... let[ting] the clutch out slowly while accelerating gently ...'. It would do so while also reducing—but usually not eliminating—automotive convulsions and learner terror. This is not the only way to unpack the material, but it was not impossibly difficult to devise. Why then is synoptic instruction so common?

It is not, as Dewey and many other critics have said, only foolish adherence to a bad habit. Synoptic teaching is deeply rooted in the ways that we learn and hold knowledge. Consider another example. If someone asks us to '... show me how you learned to swim', we typically demonstrate the end result rather than rehearsing the process by which we achieved it. We get into the pool and demonstrate how we swim, doing as well as we can. If the person who asked the question was learning to swim we usually would try especially hard to swim well because we want to demonstrate just how it is done. One can observe this aquatic equivalent of teachers' efficient mathematical problem solving in swimming pools all over the land. What is important to the accomplished performer is the finished performance, not the ways in which it was learned. Intuitively, we teach by producing such performances.

We do not carry on that way from the lack of alternatives. In principle we could instead first flounder, choke, thrash our arms and legs, and sink. Then we could swim a few strokes clumsily and stop, gasping. Then we could swim a lap quite badly, and stand panting at the end of the pool. After a pause we could swim a few laps a little better, and so on. If we proceeded in this fashion we could indeed show the questioner '... how we learned to swim,' rather than displaying the finished result. And if the questioner was trying to learn, the demonstration might have some pedagogical value.

One reason such things are so uncommon is that we generally teach as we were taught. Though learning often progresses in a fits-and-starts fashion, teachers ordinarily see the fits and starts as mistakes that must be stamped out, or 'misconceptions' that must be corrected. They rarely extend knowledge to learners in ways that capitalise on the learners' experiments, mistakes, and innovative ideas. Few teachers know how to unpack knowledge because few had teachers who did such things in school or university or professional studies. Hence when some of those learners later turn to teaching, only rarely can they draw on experience of their own that might help them to unpack knowledge for students.

Another reason, and more important here, is that it becomes more difficult to re-create and appreciate novice performance as one grows more accomplished. Few good swimmers could spontaneously reproduce their earlier incompetence, paddling as though incapable of swimming and then re-creating their progress toward solid performance. Anyone can thrash and choke, but few decent swimmers could recapture, offhand, the key difficulties that they encountered and then re-enact the crucial steps in their learning. For to learn to swim well is to un-learn the bad habits, poor attitudes, and awkwardness of beginners and poor swimmers. Such unlearning is a crucial part of learning—indeed, learning to swim well could not occur without massive un-learning. That is not unique to swimming. The more polished our performances become in any realm, the less we remember how we did things less capably, or how we thought about it. Novice performance is sometimes ingenious, but also frequently inefficient and clumsy. If we did not forget novice habits, ideas, and attitudes as we learned more, every new performance would be a struggle to learn everything all over again. Psychologists commonly think about learning as a matter of adding something, but what is subtracted is no less important. If we did not forget most elements of novice performance, life and learning would be endless repetitions. Little ever would be solidly achieved because little would be left behind. All learners would be Sysiphus.[5]

But if forgetting advances learning, it inhibits teaching. Like everyone else, most teachers have forgotten many experiences that might help them to build bridges back to those they try to teach. And like everyone else, they are encouraged to forget in part by the allure of polished performance. For to be knowledgeable and skillful is to produce polished work. The greater one's mastery, the more elegant and efficient one's performance. Mastery is something to be cherished, no less in smooth driving over a winding road than in writing an historical essay or solving a physics problem. One reason that mathematics teachers work problems as cleanly as they can is that mathematicians see elegance as a mark of good work. Stumbling through problems piecemeal seems clumsy, even though that is what mathematicians usually do on the way to cracking them. English teachers read from Twain or Hemmingway's best stories rather than some messy early draft, because that is prose of surpassing quality. It is the genuine article, the elegant writing that teachers hope students will produce and appreciate. What could be more reasonable than to launch such examples toward learners?

Another reason that teachers find it difficult to extensively unpack knowledge, then, is that polished performances are expressions of fine achievement and an essential means of communication among accomplished practitioners. Synoptic teaching often embodies crucial elements of the high culture and aspirations of a practice, be it physics or violin playing.

Still another reason that many teachers find it difficult to extensively unpack knowledge is that finished knowledge is essential for good teaching, including teaching in which knowledge is carefully unpacked. For if teachers did not know what polished work was like, they could hardly know what they want to achieve, nor could they give students examples of where learning might be headed. Without the knowledge and skill that such performances embody, teachers could never recognise signs of competent performance, inventiveness, insight, and misunderstanding among learners.[6] Despite all this, finished knowledge and appreciation of polished performance also are grave barriers to the cultivation of a practice of teaching, for they regularly blind teachers to the ways in which knowledge might be unpacked for learners' benefit.

A fourth reason that teachers infrequently unpack knowledge as they extend it is that such work is time consuming, messy, and demanding. For when teachers extend knowledge in ways that offer students many routes into it, they increase the complexity of instruction. They enrich teaching and learning but they also multiply uncertainty. Instruction becomes more difficult and the demands on teachers' knowledge, skill, and attention increase. In contrast, when teachers extend knowledge in tightly compressed form they reduce the complexity of knowledge and extending it, they constrain the uncertainties of instruction, and they limit the attentiveness required to teach.

Conceptions of knowledge

Though teachers extend knowledge in dramatically different ways, knowledge is not a neutral material that teachers transmit. It must be construed somehow to be taught or learned, and teachers construe it in radically different ways. Some treat it as though it was established, objective facts and procedures, while others treat knowledge as though it was contested and constructed. Such differences have an enormous influence on the material teachers launch toward learners. Many teachers and students of history act as though historical knowledge was an objective record of What Happened, a view that also has been familiar among historians and philosophers of history. The tracks of the past are out there, waiting to be dug up, dusted off, and set down. Writing history is seen as an objective reconstruction, and the historian's assignment is to reconstruct with a minimum of marring, scarring, and distortion. The better their work, the closer to Truth they will get. But in another line of thought and practice knowledge of the past is viewed as an imaginative construction. Historians weave knowledge from their interpretations of artifacts and documents, their inferences from what contemporaries thought happened (which in turn usually were woven out of what others thought and said), and from their analyses of other observers' accounts. On this view, knowledge is not out there to be found but is created as the mind searches for sense in ambiguous experience. Historians construct accounts of the past that are plausible, elegant, useful, or some combination of these. They achieve truths of a sort, but they are partial, contested and ephemeral.[7] Where some see discoveries others see inventions.[8]

Teachers' conceptions of knowledge also differ in the ways that they compose them. Knowledge in most fields comprises several elements: distinctive methods of inquiry and operations; special terminology; approaches to problem setting; and means of defending results.[9] To know any field implies that one knows something of all four elements. I could not plausibly claim to know arithmetic if I knew the signs and symbols but could perform none of the operations they entail, could not set or at least recognise arithmetical problems, nor somehow defend any answers I might produce. But if all elements play some part in knowing a field, teachers and investigators assign them radically different roles and weights. Some give pride of place to terminology and methods of inquiry while others focus extensively on the defence of results. Some focus only on one or two elements while others try to balance all four. Such compositional variations add up to different conceptions of what it means to know a field, and thus to very different versions of the knowledge that teachers extend to learners.

For instance, many US elementary school teachers regularly give the lion's share of mathematics instruction over to special terminology and distinctive methods and operations. They focus on identifying the operations that the '+' sign calls for, and practising them. They give no attention to the defence of results, and instead of attending to problem setting, they accept problems as they are given in texts and worksheets.[10] In contrast, some other teachers devote a great deal of attention to setting problems and defending one's work. They present stories or puzzles that have quantitative elements, encourage students to transform those elements into mathematical problems, and discuss whether the formulations make mathematical sense. Special terminology and methods play an important role in their work, but they are embedded within instruction about problem setting and defence of results.

Knowledge is composed in many different ways depending on which of these elements are given featured billing, and how many elements are in the foreground. The variety of knowledge that teachers can extend is especially dazzling when we consider that compositional differences interact with differences in the ways teachers construe knowledge. For example, many mathematics teachers attend to the defence of results as well as distinctive terminology and special methods, but they do so procedurally—i.e., they treat proof as a matter of checking with authority. They tell students to check their answers against the sheet posted in the hall, or the list at the end of the text chapter. If there is a dispute they refer students to the text or to the answer sheet, or to other books on mathematics. In contrast, a few mathematics teachers treat the defence of results as a key part of making mathematical sense and interpreting mathematical ideas. They present problems that may challenge students' efforts to defend their answers and they help students to learn to justify their answers in ways that make mathematical sense. They cultivate students' capacity to make persuasive mathematical arguments, and they treat teaching and learning about the difference between mathematically defensible and indefensible justifications as no less important than methods and results.

Such differences bear on teachers' capacity to cultivate a practice of teaching. If math teachers focus chiefly on such things as identifying the operations that the '+' sign calls for and showing students how to perform them, they need not cultivate a very complex practice of teaching. For when they extend simplified mathematical knowledge, include little on problem setting, proof, or justification of results, or treat proof as a matter of checking with authority, they constrain the complexity of knowledge and limit the attentiveness required for instruction. They do convey some of the knowledge that mathematicians have produced, but the knowledge is what Dewey termed 'inert'; it is the mechanical result of inquiry entirely divorced from the practice of inquiry in which it was produced, criticised and revised. Teachers who extend such knowledge need not think deeply about the mathematics involved, or about the ways in which they design it for learners. In contrast, when teachers frame lessons that invite students to discern the mathematical elements in a story, or to develop mathematical justifications for their work, they increase the complexity of the knowledge that they extend and the attention required to teach. Such things expand the demands on teachers' knowledge and skill, and require that they cultivate a more complex practice of teaching.

These differences in knowledge and knowledge extension also affect the limits that teachers draw around their work. When the defence of results is treated mechanically, teachers and students need only check their work against knowledge that is already given. That constrains the defence of results, limits uncertainty, and eases the difficulty of teaching and learning. But when the defence of results is treated as a matter of making good arguments, teachers and students must construct or reconstruct the foundations of knowledge as part of their work together. That complicates the knowledge with which students and teachers deal, it multiplies uncertainty, and increases the difficulty of instruction.

Interactions

As I compose this piece it is easy to distinguish between how teachers hold knowledge and how they launch it toward learners, but when I teach, the two are tangled together. The tangles often seem puzzling. For instance, many professors who teach that learners make their own sense of things also extend those ideas synoptically, as though believing they could construct knowledge for their students. Conversely, some teachers who hold knowledge as though it were fixed and objective nonetheless take care to unpack it for students. One must take account of those entanglements in order to understand the role that knowledge plays in teaching; while they often strike observers as inconsistent they make sense if one considers the demands of teaching.

Table 1 displays several ways in which teachers combine conceptions of knowledge with means of knowledge extension. In the most familiar approach, teachers hold knowledge as fixed and extend it in synoptic form (cell 1).[11] For instance, in most US elementary schools mathematics is treated as an edifice of terms, facts, and procedures that can best be extended to students in finished little clumps of rules and numerical procedures. In such cases many teachers teach two-digit multiplication by standing at the board, beginning with a 'simple' problem like 12 × 12, and saying something like this:

> The first step is to multiply 12 × 2, then write the partial product 24. The next step is to multiply 1 × 12 (if you don't know these things review your times tables), and then write that partial product. Be sure to notice that this product is indented one space from the right. Remember it; that's where lots of people go wrong. Then add the two partial products to get the answer.

Multiplication is extended toward students in a few quick, compressed gulps: knowledge of problem recognition, of the 'times tables', of rules about how to line up partial products and, with larger numbers, of rules about carrying. Teachers offer learners tightly-packed and one-dimensional packages of facts, procedures, and methods.

Such work is as familiar in universities as in elementary schools. The mathematics is more advanced, but it is extended in the same sort of dense, finished, packages of rules and procedures. Teaching of this sort is familiar in all fields of knowledge. Many history instructors launch highly compressed historical narratives at learners. To know history is to know such strings of events, and to teach history is to extend them

Table 1. Interactions between conceptions of knowledge and modes of knowledge extension

MEANS OF EXTENSION	CONCEPTIONS OF KNOWLEDGE	
	Fixed	Constructed
Synoptic	(1) Teachers extend facts and procedures in highly compressed form. They use few examples, representations, and the like.	(2) Teachers extend interpretive constructions in highly compressed form. They use few examples, representations, etc.
Unpacked	(3) Teachers extend facts and procedures in expanded form. They use examples, illustrations, etc.	(4) Teachers extend interpretive constructions in expanded form. They use many different representations, illustrations, etc.

to students. To learn history is to remember such narrative strings. In teaching about the Holocaust an instructor of this sort might offer a brief list of leading Holocaust events interspersed with statistics on camps, deaths, and trains. Knowledge can seem one-dimensional and remote, but the pace and vividness of presentations varies within such teaching. Historical narratives can be delivered in a deadpan fashion or in lively tones. But differences in tone do not change the narrative content or the conception of history. Similarly, routinised and synoptic mathematics teaching can be framed in a drab succession of workbook problems or in quick and lively presentations. Neither the knowledge nor the means of extending it change, but the pace and colour of teaching do.

At the other extreme are teachers who view knowledge as constructed and unpack it for learners (cell 4). In teaching two-digit multiplication such teachers would try to make the conceptual structure of the operations apparent, but they could do so in many different ways. They might represent the numerical operations in less abstract form by drawing twelve groups of twelve dots each on the board, or asking students to fashion their own representations of the operation. Or they might give students dried beans to represent problems like 12×12 on their desks or the floor. They might invite students to explain their representations of multiplication, and perhaps even to defend their mathematical authenticity. Or they might assign readings or computer-video materials that dealt with how what we call multiplication was handled earlier in the history of mathematics, or in other number systems. Some of these representations would convey the problem more graphically or concretely than the abstract numerical statement, while others would present alternative approaches to the numerical procedures.

Whatever the particulars, teachers of this sort extend knowledge in a variety of forms: They present examples, make analogies, use metaphors, invent alternative depictions, and the like. In these ways and others they offer instances that will give students somewhat different ways into the material and different perspectives on it. Taken alone, each representation offers students somewhat different materials with which to build bridges into multiplication, but taken together they increase learners' opportunities to 'criss-cross' the same terrain from somewhat different perspectives, and thus to gain insight into the conceptual structure of multiplication. For when students explore multiplication re-presented as groups of beans on the floor, sets of dots on the board, and the numerical version of 12 × 12, some will begin to figure out the relations among these instances—i.e., to understand 'what goes on' in multiplication, and to relate it to the standard algorithm. Teachers might then ask students to explain in what ways these were the same problem and in what ways they were different, and probe their answers. Or they might set the alternative representations out on the board and lecture about their similarities and differences. Or they might ask students to write the 12 × 12 problem in as many different numerical ways as they could, and then discuss the similarities and differences among these versions. In each of these cases teachers would offer students opportunities to make connections within and about multiplication. And they would do so by reconstructing mathematical inventions and discourse, or by inviting students to reconstruct the inventions and devise mathematical discourse. As teachers extend materials with which students can make mathematical judgments they also begin to open the practice of mathematical inquiry to students.

History is entirely different from mathematics, but certain elements in teachers' approaches would be similar. In teaching the Holocaust, instructors might supplement lectures with photographs of the camps, or readings from prisoners' journals or newspaper stories of the period. Or they might ask students to read official documents in which the Final Solution was defined and implemented. Or they might have students watch Nazi propaganda films or American newsreels, or listen to recorded interviews with Nazi officials. In such teaching, each instance of the Holocaust presents a different dimension of that sad phenomenon; the past speaks in many different voices and appears in many different perspectives. If students view photographs of death camps, read prisoners' recollections, watch documentaries and Nazi propaganda, many will make connections among these versions of the Holocaust. Teachers often encourage such work with assignments that are designed to provoke students to grapple with the meaning of the material. For example, a teacher might compile two sets of official documents concerning the Final Solution—German and British—and lecture about the different views that they contain. Or she might make copies and invite students to compare the views that they present and to write analyses of the differences. Or she might invite students to compare prisoners' diaries and recollections with the recollections of concentration camp guards, or read from Primo Levi's accounts of life, death, and occasional survival in concentration camps, or in Nazi-occupied Eastern Europe, and ask students to write about what it was like to be in a freight car on the way to a death camp, as it was depicted in Andre Schwartz-Bart's novel, *The Last of The Just*. In these and other efforts teachers would create opportunities for students to make connections within and about history, by inviting them to make historical judgments or to probe discourse about such judgments. As teachers extend materials with which students can make judgments about the past, they create occasions in which students can apprentice themselves as historical inquirers.[12]

Teachers who unpack knowledge as sketched here open many opportunities to connect teaching and learning, but such work makes formidable demands on their knowledge, skill, and other personal resources. Teachers could hardly open the practices of history or mathematics to learners unless they were at least accomplished apprentices in those practices. For no history teacher could compose the materials for the view of Holocaust history that I just sketched unless she knew the sources and was conversant with the chief interpretations; without such knowledge she would not know what materials to look for or where to find them, let alone how to frame useful assignments, or to comment thoughtfully on the materials, or deal sensibly with students' comments. Nor could teachers unpack knowledge in this way unless they had the intellectual imagination to work with diverse material, and to entertain differing or diverging perspectives on it. For in work of this sort, history is a set of competing interpretations of contested evidence; teachers could not know this version of history without at least knowing interpretations, choosing among them, and making some estimates about the evidence. Teachers who worked in these ways would have to devise a past in order to extend it to learners.

Work of this sort enriches learners' opportunities to build bridges into the material, but it also increases the difficulty and risks of instruction. When teachers extend instances of the Holocaust in many different voices, or represent multiplication in several different ways, they diversify the range of ideas and experiences that they must master, and greatly complicate the material with which they and their students must deal. The agendas of teaching and learning becomes much more dense and complex when history instructors introduce a variety of different and often divergent perspectives on events, ideas, and truth, or when multiplication is presented in several different forms. Such work often provokes puzzles about the conventional multiplication algorithm: Why must we employ it and not another? What must one know to know multiplication? Similarly, when the past is let to speak in many voices, teachers and learners must wrestle with many difficult problems of historical truth. Were the German citizens who lived near Buchenwald correct in reporting that they knew of no executions? Did Jewish prisoners perhaps exaggerate their accounts of the camps? Faced with such puzzles, students of history regularly wonder what they can know, and what really happened. Workers in every field of knowledge have means to probe such uncertainties, and even to reduce them a bit. But when knowledge is unpacked in this fashion, uncertainty is one of its most prominent features.

To extend knowledge so that learners can construct or reconstruct it thus requires considerable knowledge and many skills of explanation, analysis, presentation and re-presentation. But teachers could not work in this fashion without additional resources: the intellectual courage to manage the many uncertainties that their approach opens up, and the patience to work through complicated material so it might be made available to learners. They must be daring enough to extend knowledge in ways that are likely to increase students' difficulties, worries, and even anguish. Knowledge and skill are never enough in any sort of teaching, but the more ambitiously teachers work the more supplements to knowledge and skill they must mobilize.

These demands help to explain why many teachers extend knowledge in less taxing ways. When they extend finished knowledge of facts and procedures (cell 1) they constrain intellectual demands on themselves and students. They need only present strings of causes and effects, names and dates, procedures and facts, and students need only reproduce such material to learn. Teachers can relatively easily make connections with learning, for they extend knowledge in a crisp and clearly defined form. Many students find it easy to use such bridges, for they need only walk the straight and narrow.[13] Teachers can work in this way without much cultivating a practice of teaching, for such routinised knowledge requires little self-conscious monitoring or analysis. Teachers need not know the material deeply, and even if they do, they need not deploy such knowledge for instruction. Uncertainty and dispute are constrained when knowledge is presented as though it were unambiguous, and teachers' dependence on students is limited when they invite learners to follow a path that already is cut and plainly marked.

But teachers have other alternatives that lie between the extremes just described. One that is quite common in universities is to treat knowledge as constructed but to extend it in synoptic form (cell 2). Another, increasingly common in US elementary teaching, is to treat knowledge as fixed but to extend it in somewhat unpacked form (cell 3). These alternatives differ greatly in most respects, but they share one crucial feature: Both combine an ambitious and open approach to extending knowledge in one dimension with a conservative and tightly constrained approach on others.

Consider teachers who view knowledge as constructed but extend knowledge in tight synoptic packages (cell 2). For instance, some elementary school teachers see mathematics as matter of disciplined argument about quantity and shape, and they give special stress to problem setting and defence of results. They are keen that students learn about the intellectual structure of mathematics, but they extend their version of mathematics in polished, synoptic form. Rather than unpacking mathematics so that students can learn to make mathematical arguments themselves, teachers extend finished and highly compressed accounts of mathematical ideas. For instance, a teacher might begin the 12 × 12 problem discussed earlier by saying that:

> .... whole number multiplication procedures are just a way to combine equal groups of numbers. We could thus re-formulate the 12 × 12 problem this way: How to combine twelve groups of twelve each? Problems of this sort could be solved by repeated addition, but that is quite inefficient unless the numbers are quite small. Multiplication is more efficient. Adding x+x+x+x+x+x+x+x (however many times it is specified in 'y') is thus condensed and transformed into writing x (y).
>
> But to multiply with two-digit numbers one also must understand how numbers are put together in a system of place value. When doing the first step in this problem [multiplying 2 × 12], the multiplier [2] is from the ones place in twelve, while the multiplicand [12] is from the tens. Hence, multiplying 2x12 actually combines two different multiplications: 2 × 12 and 10 × 2. Thus in the problem's second step—multiplying what looks like 1 × 12—one actually multiplies 10 by 12. The result of that operation is 120. Though one drops the zero in writing the second partial product, we recognize it by placing the product as though the zero were written. This convention reflects the fact that in two-digit multiplication the second partial product is always in the hundreds. The last

zero need not be written, but the product must be set one place to the left of first partial product.

This version of multiplication is no less synoptic than the earlier procedural example, but the two synopses contain very different versions of mathematical knowledge. One teacher acted as though mathematics was a body of objective facts, procedures, and methods, while the other acted as though it was a way of making sense of number and quantity in which explanation of ideas was essential. The first teacher presented procedures as the core of mathematics while the second offered a thoughtful account of how procedures work, and why. The first account is far from the practice of mathematical inquiry, for only a few products of inquiry are presented. The second approach seems closer, but the practice of mathematics still remains largely hidden. Though learners are exposed to sophisticated reasoning, it is not offered in ways that permit students to make varied, active contact with the ideas. Learners must either sing along with the teacher's polished mathematical analyses or be lost.

History instructors who work in this way extend finished interpretations to students, rather than unpacking history so that students could weigh the evidence as they frame their own interpretations. Such teaching is no less synoptic than the earlier compressed narrative, but the content differs. The first version offers the Holocaust as a thin string of dates, places, and events, while the second presents a dense set of ideas about what happened and what it means. Teachers commonly refer to both as explanations of history, but the nature of explanation differs radically. In the first case it takes the form of a compressed chronology, a logic of one-thing-after-another, while in the second it takes the form of a highly compressed argument, a logic of interpretation.[14] The first version offers only a thin summary of some results of such inquiry, while the second presents a much richer example of historical argument, but offers only the polished result. The practice of inquiry—collecting and weighing evidence, making inferences about its meaning and judgments about its plausibility, generalising from the evidence, and reaching conclusions—lies behind a veil of polished conclusions.

The second approach to extending knowledge makes appreciable demands on teachers' knowledge, skill, and other resources. For in addition to knowing a subject's facts and procedures teachers also must know its conceptual structure and be able to relate the two. That considerably expands and complicates the terrain of instruction, for when knowledge is construed as a matter of argument and interpretation rather than fact and procedures, teachers must grapple with complex and often ill-structured concepts rather than simply presenting intellectual routines. The difficulty of teaching also increases, because the knowledge they extend is more uncertain. But such teaching makes few demands on teachers in the ways that they extend knowledge, for they present material in compressed form. The contents of their synopses differ radically from those who hold knowledge in procedural form, but both sorts of teaching are very compact and abstract. Teachers may perform as accomplished and even brilliant learners, but they do not unpack knowledge so that learners could explore it.[15]

Such teaching may strike observers as illogical, but it is eminently practical. For while the demands on teachers' personal resources and the range of attentiveness grow in one dimension they are constrained in another.[16] Teachers who work in this way need not struggle to expose the practice of inquiry, nor to unpack knowledge in ways that might support students' efforts to learn the practice.

A very different approach to knowledge extension is found among teachers who hold knowledge as fixed but extend it in unpacked form (cell 3). For instance, in teaching the 12 × 12 problem discussed above an instructor of this sort might combine a tightly packed procedural exposition with several re-presentations. Thus she might begin two-digit multiplication by standing at the board, beginning with a 'simple' problem like 12 × 12, and saying something like the teacher discussed earlier:

> The first step is to multiply 12 × 2, then write the partial product 24. The next step is to multiply 1 × 12 (if you don't know these things review your times tables), and then write that partial product. Be sure to notice that this product is indented one space from the right. Remember it; that's where lots of people go wrong. Then add the two partial products to get the answer.

Knowledge of mathematics here is procedural—knowledge of problem recognition, of the 'times tables', of rules about how to line up partial products, and the like. Teachers offer learners tightly-packed and one-dimensional packages of facts, procedures, and methods. But elementary teachers who hold this version of mathematical knowledge increasingly also unpack it by re-presenting the procedure with groups of beans, or sticks, or by inviting students to do so. Often teachers drill students in such re-presentations. Students thereby are given access to modestly unpacked versions of knowledge, *albeit* closely tied to drill-and-practice in procedures, rules, and facts. The alternative depictions offer a somewhat expanded way to extend multiplication along with a conventional picture of arithmetical knowledge. Though their conception of knowledge rather constrains the range of instances that they can offer, in such cases teachers do somewhat unpack the knowledge they extend.

History teachers who hold knowledge of the past as a narrative of objective facts often work in a similar fashion. They can expand the factual synopsis of Holocaust history sketched earlier by adding instances. Bare, compressed narrative is embroidered with the names of concentration camps, the general causes of Jewish and Gypsy death, the type of work that prisoners did, and the like. Such examples add something to a synoptic narrative. They open up the narrative slightly and make it a bit less compressed. They add some specifics to what was a flat and rather sparsely populated terrain, and colour it somewhat. But such narratives still are quite constrained, for the material that is added does not open up new contours in the written past. The conception of knowledge that underlies work of this sort limits both the instances that teachers could admit and the ways in which they would present them. Teachers would not, for instance, introduce *The Last of the Just*, or Primo Levi's work, for these novels would not count as historical evidence. No matter how much they had been informed by experience and even historical research, the novels are works of literary imagination, not historical research, and they would not fit with this view of historical knowledge.[17] The limited conception of knowledge that animates a view of history as established facts typically would exclude such material. Historical knowledge could be unpacked, but only within one or two dimensions.[18]

Similar cases increasingly populate the instructional landscape, as recent efforts to increase thoughtfulness in learning have stimulated the development of new instructional materials. These materials have been designed on the assumption that knowledge is constructed, and that in order to reconstruct it students should explore a rich variety of ideas. But while the new materials often improve on their traditional counterparts, the teachers who use them often continue to hold knowledge as fixed and objective. For instance, more and more reading teachers work with 'literature-based' curricula that are richer than mechanically composed basal readers; yet many treat literature in a thoroughly mechanical fashion, as though it were only selections from a traditional basal reading text. Similarly, more and more elementary teachers use a tempting array of novel graphic and concrete materials in their mathematics classes. All were designed to re-present mathematics in a rich variety of ways, and thus help teachers to build many bridges to learners. But the new materials often do not change how many teachers think about mathematics, who treat the novel materials in a rigidly procedural fashion, as if they were working with number problems on traditional worksheets.[19] Partisans of the improvements see such work as inconsistent and a perversion, but many teachers report that they like them because they offer many new ways to extend knowledge to students, and many helpful activities. Teachers use the materials with pleasure, even though their conception of knowledge constrains what they can see in them and the use they can make of them.[20]

To extend knowledge in this fashion somewhat expands the demands on teachers' knowledge, skill, and other resources. For in addition to knowing a subject's methods and procedures teachers must be familiar with a range of instances. They must additionally be able to interrelate those instances, and to intelligibly extend them. But these demands are relatively modest, for when teachers hold knowledge as fixed they unpack it only in one dimension. The instances they extend are all of a type, and they connect them either as similar cases of the same thing or in linear causal fashion. In addition, uncertainty is constrained because teachers deal with fewer arguments and interpretations, and grapple with many fewer complex or confusing concepts. Teachers build several bridges back to learners, but they are all of a single type. Hence while teaching of this sort makes some demands on teachers' personal resources, and somewhat extends the range of attentive practice, it does so only modestly.

I have touched only on a few features of a large and largely unexplored terrain. One thread in my account has been the great variability in how teachers build bridges back toward learners, depending on how they hold and extend knowledge. What counts as knowledge, as a representation, or as a connection among ideas varies dramatically depending on how teachers construe and extend knowledge. What teachers must know and do in order to extend knowledge also varies. Moreover, since much of teaching consists in ideas and the manipulation of ideas, there is no single body of technique in this profession. What some commentators refer to as the 'technical core' of education varies with the ways in which teachers hold ideas and extend them to learners. There is no uniform technology of instruction, nor any single body of 'essential' knowledge and skills for teaching. There are instead several different bodies of knowledge and skill, depending on how teachers construe knowledge and enact its extension.[21] It is difficult to see how it could be otherwise, given deep differences about the nature of knowledge and continuing uncertainty and dispute about the ends and means of instruction.

Another thread in my account concerns the relation between teaching and authentic intellectual practices. When teachers extend thin and mechanical synopses of knowledge they work at a great remove from the practices in which knowledge is produced, criticised and revised. Such teaching offers learners a few fruits of others' inquiries, but does not much help learners to cultivate the intellectual practices in which those fruits flourished. It does constrain the demands on teachers' knowledge, skill, and other personal resources. In contrast, when teachers unpack knowledge so that learners might construct or reconstruct it they open up some elements of the practices in which truths are constructed, contested and reconstructed.[22] Instead of telling inherited truths teachers extend knowledge in ways that can help learners to cultivate the capacity to establish truths, to debate truth, to learn how it is established, why it might be contested, and how those contests might rationally be decided. That richer instructional diet makes greater demands on teachers' knowledge, skill, and other resources.

But my main thread has been that the lack of many efforts to thoughtfully unpack knowledge is no simple oversight, easily remedied with a bit of supplementary instruction. For such teaching cuts against the ways that we learn and hold knowledge, and the value that we attach to masterful performance. Much deliberate re-learning would be required before most good performers in any field would be able to understand novice work and appreciate the paths to competent performance. Much study of learning would be required in order to recover the elements of early and inexpert performance, and to learn what instructional approaches might help novices to improve. Much analysis of knowledge and of teaching would be required to understand how knowledge might be unpacked and extended so as to offer learners greater access to it. Many opportunities to cultivate intellectual courage and adventurousness would be required if teachers were to learn to extend knowledge in ways that increased uncertainty and multiplied the difficulty of instruction.

Teachers also would have to acquire a sort of double vision about knowledge itself: they would have to distance themselves from their own finished knowledge in order to learn how to extend what they know in more various and less finished ways, yet they would have to use finished knowledge to guide and inform that teaching. Learning to hold and use knowledge in such very different ways at once is essential to cultivating a sophisticated practice of teaching, but it is no mean feat.

Acknowledgements

My thanks to Deborah Loewenburg Ball, Magdalene Lampert, and Suzanne Wilson for helpful comments on earlier versions of this contribution.

Notes

1. Few psychologists have represented learning and teaching in this way. One appeal of Lev Vygotsky's ideas is that he portrayed learning and teaching as processes of 'scaffolding', in

which teachers and learners create cognitive structures that support learners' formulations and make it possible for them to push ahead. Vygotsky's ideas were in marked contrast to the main line of US psychological thought, for until recently psychologists tended to view teaching as presenting the stimuli and inducing the responses that would produce learning. See L. Vygotsky, *Thought and Language*, ed. and trans. E. Hanfmann and G. Vakar, Cambridge, MASS, MIT Press. The best secondary account is Wertsh. J. V., *Vygotsky and the Social Formation of Mind*. Cambridge, MASS, Harvard University Press, 1985.

2. In writing about instructional performances I assume that they are jointly produced by students and teachers, though I do not always repeat that qualification. Instructional performances are jointly constructed even when some students' contribution is disruptive, or a passive and withdrawn consent not to disrupt. I use the term instruction in that sense, to refer to jointly conducted practices of learning and teaching, even if conducted at a distance. Teachers usually have the lead role in these joint productions, but that does not mean that they have the most important role; students do the learning, after all, and instruction affects students as well as teachers, and each through the other.
3. Dewey, J., *The Child and the Curriculum*, Chicago, University of Chicago Press, first published 1902, reprinted 1973. Like many of his predecessors and later thinkers, Dewey thought it no great task to solve this problem. Once knowledge was re-cast from a developmentally suitable perspective it would be accessible to learners. Dewey was correct in seeing that finished knowledge is a great problem in teaching and learning. But his view that the problem was simply the result of foolish inherited ideas and habits was not.
4. Sir Michael Polanyi elegantly discussed tacit knowledge in *Personal Knowledge* (Chicago, University of Chicago Press, 1958) though he does not take up the difficulties it entails for teaching and learning.
5. Few American learning theorists seem to have noticed that learning requires forgetting, or unlearning. I suspect that inattention to this matter was due to at least two things. One was the tabula rasa conception of mind that most English-speaking psychologists embraced. For if the mind is regarded as an empty vessel, then the problem of learning is to figure out how the mind gets filled, or filled effectively or efficiently. Only if one sees the mind as constantly trying to make sense of things might the problem of learning include how more efficient or effective sense-making supplants less-effective thought. Un-learning would be part of such supplanting. Another reason that American psychologists ignored forgetting probably was their American belief that learning, and hence teaching, were easy.
6. In US elementary schools such teaching often is no more than a compressed version of knowledge that is mechanically held. But even then, it serves the same normative and instructional guidance purposes as more sophisticated knowledge.
7. Arguments of this sort divide philosophers who specialise in the theory of knowledge, and they divide specialists within particular disciplines. They broke out in all the academic disciplines in the late 19th and early 20th centuries, and have been carried on down to the present. Generally on these developments in European thought, see H. Stuart Hughes, *Consciousness and Society: The Reorientation of European Social Thought*, Cambridge, MASS, Harvard University Press, 1958.
8. These differences in how knowledge is construed have been variously characterised. Commentators in education use terms like rote, procedural, and mechanical at one extreme, and understanding, making sense, or higher order thinking at the other. But the differences are difficult to define plainly, even at the extremes, for students 'understand' mathematics even when they learn it as mechanical memorization, though they understand it differently and less deeply than when they learn it as ideas about number and shape that they must explain and defend within certain mathematically legitimate terms of reference. And the definitional difficulties increase when one tries to grapple with the many cases in which teachers or students fashion some combination of the extreme approaches. My aim is not to frame tight definitions; I want to explore the ways in which different constructions of knowledge affect how knowledge is

extended. Hence I am willing to accept fairly rough and ready characterizations of the different ways in which knowledge is construed.

9. Special methods or techniques of a field include such things as the archival or demographic techniques of historians, and the methods of textual analysis in literary criticism. From this angle, teaching arithmetic entails presenting such things as column addition, or explaining that operation by analogy to counting on, or both. Similarly, teaching literary criticism might include presenting definitions of textual analysis, or giving examples of it, or demonstrating how it is done, or some combination of these. Specialised language or technical terminology comprises, in mathematics, signs and symbols, and terms like addition, factoring, etc. In literature it includes such terms as character, plot, and meter. The special language of physics includes mass, acceleration, and electron. From this perspective, to teach literature is to define or describe plots, or both. And to teach arithmetic is to define the meaning of '+,' or to present examples of what it entails, or to compare it with such other terms as '–'.

   Problem-setting entails defining questions in ways that can be productively handled within the field. In classical mechanics, physicists set problems with a special sort of abstraction: from many attributes of bodies in motion, they construct a few unusual attributes that permit calculation of acceleration, force, and mass. Hence to teach this sub-field of physics might be to illustrate how problems are set up, or to present alternative but unproductive ways of setting them up. Historians also set problems, but because much historical evidence is thin, fragmentary, and ambiguous, framing problems often requires more than tight definitions and salient questions. Setting problems for historical inquiry usually requires close familiarity with the evidence, and the exercise of judgment about how it may connect with narrative or argument. From this angle, then, teaching history might include demonstrations of how to work with archival sources to set up problems for research, or analyses of other scholars' well and weakly framed research problems, or both.

   The defence of what one thinks one might know is also an element of most fields. Each contains an array of means by which inquirers can check on their own doubt about a result, or respond to the challenge: Prove it! Suppose, for instance, that a student doubts her solution to a multiplication problem, and asks her teacher if it is correct. Teaching arithmetic in this case may include showing the student how to 'prove' her answer—i.e., divide the product by one of the numbers multiplied, and see if the quotient is identical to the other number multiplied. Or the teacher could tell the student to check the answer against the list at the end of the chapter. Similarly, many teachers show their students how to defend historical knowledge by reference to established authorities—i.e., by checking facts and conclusions against reference works or texts—while others give examples of how to assess the consistency between evidence and argument, or consistency within evidence and within arguments, or both.

10. One-sided approaches to knowledge composition are not the special preserve of little children and their teachers. An example can be found in graduate education in the social sciences, which often commences with a heavy dose of 'methodology', or 'methods of research'. In such courses students regularly are introduced to academic fields and disciplines as though their central feature were the special techniques and terms of inquiry. Problem setting and defence of results are frequently ignored, or treated as equivalent to deciding the appropriate approach to data collection and analysis. Many novice practitioners in the social sciences conclude that methodology is the most important feature of their practice. Some go on to accord it very special status, in the foreground of their work. But there is nothing utterly unique about methodology in this connection: Any element of a field can be given such prominence.

11. The alternative approaches to knowledge extension depicted in this table are sometimes referred to under other rubrics: Presentation and explanation are the most familiar. But it is not helpful for my purposes to rely on explanation as the presenting category. For, as will become clear, explanation varies greatly across the approaches arrayed in this table. The categories I use are only a beginning in this large and little explored area, and doubtless could be improved. But they are at least a little less rubbery, and a bit more closely connected to the actual operations

of knowledge extension, than most established terms. Additionally, the alternatives sketched in this table should not be mistaken for a broader list of possible approaches to teaching itself. For they do not take account of other important influences, such as the ways that teachers organise discourse or acquaint themselves with students' knowledge.

12. Teachers who work in this fashion pursue several sorts of connections. One is between instances that are more particular or concrete and those that are more general or abstract. Offering both graphic and concrete re-presentations of the 12 x 12 problem would increase many students' opportunities to grasp the content of the standard abstract numerical depiction of the problem, by depicting it in several less abstract ways. Each of these opportunities could help students to make some of the connections that may be entailed in a grasp of multiplication. Similarly, familiarity with many different manifestations of the Holocaust would help many students to frame and thoughtfully assess generalisations about that episode of European history.

    A second sort of connection is among different perspectives on the same matter. As history teachers show photographs of the Nazi death camps, read aloud from prisoners' journals, invite students to read Primo Levi, *Survival in Auschwitz* (trans. Stuart Woolfe, New York, Touchstone Press, 1996), or *The Last of the Just*, and show the documentary film 'Shoah' (dir. Claude Lanzmann, France, 1985), or Nazi propaganda films and American newsreels, they confront students with very different sorts of knowledge of the Holocaust, with several different perspectives on the events and with some rather different notions of what is true of those events. The differences and disjunctions offer occasions to compare visions, to understand differences and similarities in historical knowledge, and perhaps to attempt resolutions. Such connections make it possible for learners to deepen and enrich their knowledge of a field.

    Still another sort of connection is between extant and new knowledge. Learning, after all, is partly a matter of building out from what is already known. Learners use what already is in hand to help make sense of new material. For instance, when teachers represent the multiplication of 12 × 12 as repeated addition they open a possible bridge from established to new knowledge. The re-presentation offers learners a way to build from addition, with which they would be familiar, toward multiplication, about which they ordinarily would know little. It also offers them an opportunity to understand the relations between multiplication and addition, and to appreciate the greater economy of multiplication for certain problems. These connections are not mutually exclusive—indeed, they often overlap. But each sort is essential to learners' efforts to cultivate deep understanding of a field.

13. Such work is especially easy because this version of knowledge is an old and familiar staple of both scholastic and popular culture in the USA. It is what most teachers were taught, and what many students learn outside of school. Hence they need make no basic intellectual changes to teach or learn.

14. That difference is not a matter of how much teachers know, but of how they hold knowledge. Among those who construe history as an objective record of human events, some have a rich command of the material while others have only a superficial grasp. And while some teachers who embrace a constructivist view of history are enormously learned, others are not. These differences in depth of knowledge influence the quality of what teachers extend to students, but they need not affect its synoptic character.

15. Not surprisingly, learners often respond to interpretive synopses by treating them as though they were mere procedures. They learn to reproduce the interpretations, but do not raise questions about the ideas, nor apply them to related material.

16. These differences in teaching of this sort are not necessarily a consequence of how much teachers know. Many well-informed university instructors extend knowledge of calculus in a synoptic, facts-and-procedures fashion, while others who are mathematically no more knowledgeable teach the same subject in highly interpretive but equally synoptic ways. Nor does my account imply anything about how teachers hold knowledge apart from instruction. Mathematicians who teach calculus as a synopsis of facts and procedures often embrace a constructivist

perspective in their research. I am concerned only with how teachers hold and extend knowledge for instruction.

17. The same restraints would apply to film, even perhaps to 'documentary' films like 'Shoah', for it is also a work of imagination.
18. Many more instances could be added to such an account—i.e., the number of machine-gun shells that captive Jews manufactured, the average number of victims that died each week between 1942 and 1945, how many freight cars were used to transport them, and so on. Or teachers could assign archival research, and invite students to use original sources. They might ask students to write a factual narrative of events based on the sources. Or they might invite students to use the sources to critique the accuracy of some other narrative history of the events. Work of this sort would make the Holocaust somewhat more accessible, by further populating the historical terrain, and opening it up somewhat. But the material would still remain one-dimensional. For no matter how vigorously teachers added examples in the narrative above, the contours of history would remain roughly the same—i.e., a linear recital of facts.
19. See the cases in the Fall 1990 issue of *Educational Evaluation and Policy Analysis*, for examples and discussion of such work. See also Cuban, L., *How Teachers Taught* (New York, Longmans, 1984).
20. Cuban, L., *How Teachers Taught* (New York, Longmans, 1984).
21. Hence what Lee Shulman terms pedagogical content knowledge (the knowledge of how to represent particular subject matter to learners) also varies with conceptions of knowledge and means of extending it to learners (see L. Shulman, Knowledge and Teaching: The Foundations Of the New Reform, *Harvard Educational Review*, 57(1), 1–22). None of these bodies of knowledge and skill are particularly well-developed, though researchers have made some progress in documenting the elements of effective 'direct instruction' (which is comprised in cells 1 and 3 of Table 1) since the mid-1970s. Further progress in developing the alternatives could advance teaching and the understanding of teaching.
22. Differences in teachers' conceptions of knowledge reflect or parallel disputes within disciplines, and in more general philosophical discourse, about the nature of knowledge and how truth is established. It has become almost a commonplace in modern philosophy that knowledge is a construction, even a convenient fiction, a view that also has had some popularity in literature, history, and the arts. Even in mathematics and physics, which once seemed bastions of certainty, knowledge is now widely regarded as a system of mental constructs, less an objective representation of a real world than an imaginative or even artistic construction of possible worlds. Many scientists say that they value their theories as much for their elegance or imagination as for their explanatory power. Some scientists and philosophers insist that in this respect science has much in common with the humanities or the arts (see recent Swiss physicist's book on origins of the universe, and sub-atomic physics). But if these ideas have become increasingly fashionable, they still are vigorously contested. Dissenting commentators regularly argue that knowledge is a more or less accurate representation of things as they are. And, even more impressive, the disciplinary practice of the scientific modernists seems to differ little from those who hold more traditional views. Scientists and sociologists, like historians and modernist literary critics often write as though what they know is true, and that it can be communicated to others who will apprehend it—whatever their theories of knowledge. In this matter as in so many others, practice seems to contest theory.

Postscript: The spirit of the age

Stuart Maclure
London, UK

This contribution provides a brief endpiece to the Special Issue in honour of Harry Judge from the point of view of a journalist active over much of the period discussed. It focuses particularly on two papers concerned with teacher training in the UK and USA.

It is my privilege to contribute a brief endpiece to this collection of papers—not as an academic participant but as a journalist who watched the educational drama unfold from an editorial chair in the stalls. My comments are prompted by two major contributions to this collection which go directly to the central theme of the education and training of teachers: Sir William Taylor's discussion of the James Committee and Harry Judge's part in its deliberations as shown by the committee's working papers; and Professor Patricia Albjerg Graham's synoptic account of teacher training in the United States since the 1960s.

For me, these two articles—very different in form but covering much of the same ground—provide a running counterpoint to the main theme. They both show how changes in the wider social and political background influenced policy-making and determined what was and was not possible at the end of the 1960s when Mrs Thatcher set up the James Committee.

First, it has to be acknowledged that there were major practical difficulties to be overcome, many of which would call for strong executive action. The teacher training colleges/colleges of education were in a state of turmoil after a decade of break-neck expansion. Student numbers had doubled. There had been a corresponding increase in training college staff. While there was no indication that entry qualifications had fallen, it was obvious that what the colleges most needed was a period of stability and consolidation—and equally obvious that this was unlikely to be among the options on offer.

The university education departments were busy digesting the administrative changes which had come in the wake of the Robbins Report. And on both sides of the

Atlantic, staff in these departments were actively trying to raise their standing with their academic specialist peers. Because 'education' *per se* was not generally regarded as a credible academic study, for many this meant focusing on underlying subjects like psychology and sociology and seeking recognition in those fields rather than in activities directly related to the training of future professional teachers.

Second, policy-making was made more difficult by uncertainties inside the Department of Education and Science about wider government policy. Some of these were recurring preoccupations which varied in severity year by year like the demography of future supply and demand. In 1971, when the James Committee sat, doubts about demographic factors were a major consideration. The Government was unwilling to give the James Committee any clear guidance on numbers or finance, and the final report was undermined for this reason.

At the heart of the James concerns was the role of the universities in the professional training of teachers. Lord James himself had his own doubts, which inclined him to support a separate first academic cycle with separate arrangements in the second and third cycles for professional training. But in the Department of Education and Science, the incorporation of teacher training within the higher education college structure came to be seen as a necessary way of dealing with the inflated numbers in the training colleges. Thus policy, not yet fully articulated, foreclosed options the James Committee were considering. There was, of course, nothing unusual about the way policy bowed to circumstances. A decade earlier the excellent decision to extend the training college course from two years to three was taken because of a short-lived and misconceived fear that there might otherwise be a shortage of jobs for teachers in primary schools when the 'bulge' had passed through.

The differences between the James Committee and the DES were important because they were linked to the way the James Committee was set up. The DES had long fended off the setting up of an inquiry. By the time Mrs Thatcher decided to fulfil her election pledge the model of the National Advisory Councils had gone out of fashion in the face of changes in the style of government away from administration towards active management. The suspicion must be that the last thing the Department wanted was 'independent' advice: the hope was that a full-time group of outsiders, working under the watchful eye of senior DES officials, would provide external endorsement for whatever it was the Department intended to do. Things did not work out like that because the Department was not ready to give the Committee the necessary steers and the Committee had a mind of its own.

By the end of the 1960s, management was seen as the future, administration as the past. This came out clearly in the 1970s with the reform of local government and the emergence of corporate management as a means of bringing education more firmly within the corporate net at local level. For teacher training it meant pressure to centralise control of the system—a process which only came to fruition in the 1980s. A new management style replaced the old consultative mechanisms which had become a platform for the exponents of the *status quo*. In accordance with the law of unintended consequences, the reform of local government finance made it harder for the Department to manage that part of the system which came within the orbit of local government but the pressure to centralise continued.

With the all-seeing eye of hindsight we can now see that the late 1960s and the early 1970s signalled a major change in public attitudes towards education. It was the beginning of the Great Reaction against the perceived excesses of the 1960s summed up in the idea of 'the permissive society' and ending in rampant student revolt in the Paris of May 1968.

Looking back on those interesting times it becomes clear that 1970—a quarter of a century after the end of the Second World War—was a momentous year of change. It was like the fulcrum on which the educational see-saw was perched. It marked a sharp and radical change from optimism to pessimism, from confidence to doubt, from public pride in the post-war education system to a sudden loss of faith in the schools and the teachers. Of course it was more complicated than this. Those questioned in opinion polls were quite likely to praise the teachers at the school their children attend while joining in the criticism of every one else. But who said public opinion had to be scrupulously logical? There had been a shift in the priorities. It was articulated by a right-wing coterie but it touched on something much deeper.

Eric Hoyle and Peter John summed up the accusation brought against the educators in an article in the *Oxford Review of Education* in 1998. 'Not too oversimply,' they wrote, 'it was that during the sixties the teacher training institutions, staffed predominantly by child-centred and left-inclined lecturers, produced a generation of teachers lacking classroom skills, imbued with egalitarianism, and unwilling to inculcate an appropriate work ethic in their pupils' (Hoyle & John, 1998, p. 69).

The only evidence quoted was anecdotal, of the kind familiar to readers of the *Daily Mail*, but there is no doubt many people believed it including many on the Labour side of the political fence. It certainly rang a bell inside James Callaghan's private office and played a part in the framing of the Ruskin College speech of 1976. Evidence from public examinations did not support the sweeping charges, nor did the Plowden Report which had appeared in 1967 and gave the primary schools a measured vote of confidence. A scatter-gun attack on bad teaching practices could not be proved or disproved by the available evidence (though HMI in their careful observation of real classrooms gave no credit to these blanket criticisms).

As for the political complexion of teachers at all levels in the system, a National Opinion Poll commissioned by the *TES* and the *THES* provided information about their voting intentions in the October 1974 General Elections. Of the total sample, the Conservative share came out at 37% as against 30% for Labour and 27% for the Liberals. A breakdown of voting intentions by type of institution showed a somewhat different picture: 44% per cent of primary teachers would choose the Conservatives and only 23% Labour. Teachers in colleges were divided fairly equally between the competing parties, with the Liberals the largest percentage group. Among the polytechnics and the universities, the Conservatives had the least support, 24% and 23% respectively. The assumed left-wing inclination of university and polytechnic staff was borne out, but there was nothing specifically on academics in Education Departments.

But the truth or falsehood of the accusations was much less important than the way they resonated with the media and with the politicians. The public mood had changed and the politicians made haste to respond. Education had become a major topic for political argument and electioneering. And so began the bi-party traverse which led in due course to the Ruskin speech of 1976 and the Education Reform Act a decade later.

The teacher trainers were in a particularly exposed position. The educational psychologists and sociologists had only recently scored a monumental success. Their patient research had demolished the credibility of the selection procedures required to operate the eleven-plus and provided the evidence which persuaded non-partisan educational opinion to go along with the Crosland initiative in 1965. Now the public mood had changed. The sociologists continued to investigate the links between social class and educational performance, but there was neither the will nor the capacity for reform on the scale which might have radically altered the social environment in which the schools had to work. Doing something about class divisions was a matter of long-term social development far beyond the remit of public education. It seemed much more sensible for the schools to concentrate on those ways of improving educational performance by more effective teaching and learning which lay within their grasp. Patricia Graham's essay describes how the politics and priorities of teacher education in the United States moved from the Sputnik era of academic involvement in curriculum reform to the introduction of programmes aimed at the underprivileged (another euphemism of those days)—and how the sociological hopes for education as an agent of social change and greater equality faded when Coleman and Jencks exposed how little could be achieved within the bounds of what was politically practicable.

There were many reasons for more central intervention to bring back into the public domain aspects of education which had become the preserve of the teachers. It was quite understandable why the government and parliament might wish to take a bigger part in the setting of priorities. There was an increasing interest in what became known as the core curriculum (though few people thought in terms of a statutory 'national curriculum'). What happened in the seventies was that education became much more interesting to politicians and this naturally strengthened the instincts of government to take control. As the responsibilities of government expanded so too did the government's accountability for their discharge of a wider range of activities. The idea of an omni-competent government is absurd but politically irresistible and the electoral system ensures that it ends in tears at irregular intervals. But it is powerful political medicine and leads to questions like, 'why doesn't the Government do something about obesity?' and stop dogs savaging children.

Such reflections lead quickly to the quick-sands where angry old men flounder. But questions about the mind-set of teacher trainers raised in caricature by the right-wing critics of the 1970s are important and will not go away. Is there a necessary liberal agenda for teacher education? Are there common characteristics of temperament and social inclination among those who make educating the teachers their vocation? How far do the political assumptions built into public education rub off on teachers in the form of ideals which have political consequences? Do particular academic disciplines and particular professions tend in particular political directions? And if so, does it matter and is there any acceptable away in which to alter these predispositions?

Or do these differences about values simply have to be accommodated within the larger set of competing ideas which are needed to make a liberal education system work in an open democracy? There are few absolutes—a slogan like Equality of Opportunity conveniently slurs over the conflict between Equality and Opportunity. Given the part competition plays as a spur to endeavour in sport and commerce it is unlikely that it can, let alone should, be excluded from what goes on in schools. It is the job of teachers to manage the tensions between the interests of different pupil groups. Any working definition of inconclusiveness has to recognise that this means internal contradictions and an ability to live with ambiguity and compromise. Learning about these tensions should be a major aim of a student training to be a teacher.

There are obvious differences between the culture of public education and that of independent schools. These cannot be reconciled by government: both contribute to the preparation of students for higher education and the professions. This is the can of worms which moved Sir Keith Joseph and his successors to bring teacher training under tight control, not a suspected left-wing conspiracy. Conservative Ministers compared the culture of public education with that of the independent schools which they thought were more oriented towards study and the achievement of academic success. They wished the maintained schools to be more achievement-oriented and wanted teacher training to be geared to their ideas on curriculum and methods. It is notable that when Labour succeeded the Conservatives in 1997 little happened to change the politics of education.

The change in the relationship between politicians and educators across the board is now a fact of life. It does not seem to be at all unreasonable for politicians to be interested in the priorities of schooling. A by-product of the Great Reaction was a perceived need to re-emphasise the school's traditional role and raise the priority given to effective instruction and learning. The years when responsibility for deciding these priorities were effectively ceded to the schools themselves can now be seen as a lengthy aberration. Unfortunately the managers at the centre have decided to work through detailed prescription and targets. This ensures some immediate success but has proved to be excessively bureaucratic and will be counter-productive if it removes the professional elbow-room of good teachers.

One thing which is lacking is the kind of intelligent intelligence-gathering once provided by Her Majesty's Inspectorate. The desire for a new regime of regular testing swept away the old HMI system and replaced it with Ofsted and a much more limited role for less carefully selected inspectors and more hostile manners. Present discussion of in-service training cannot ignore the important post-experience training courses run by the old HMI. The Inspectorate's work was important in this respect. But, of course, charismatic HMIs like Robin Tanner and Christian Schiller were also tarred with the progressive brush. Their example served as a warning: it was to be no part of the modern system of curriculum management to employ a cadre of independent and respected HMI whose attitudes could not easily be controlled.

What is clear, however, is that the Education Department lost out by removing HMI from inside the Department and handing the survivors over to Ofsted. In former times HMIs had been at the heart of policy-making in the Department, available along the corridor with the senior civil servants, to be brought into discussion when needed. Life for former senior chief inspectors like Sheila Browne or Eric Bolton would not have been easy if they had continued to act as independent advisers inside the Department after Kenneth Baker's nationalising Reform Bill, but if they had been there Ministers might have had a better idea about what their directives would mean on the ground. One incidental consequence of the way HMI was set up was that it provided the Department with a memory, something which appears to be lacking as the wheel of bright ideas turns round and round.

Questions about academic freedom lie near the surface of any such discussion of the control of teacher training but the universities have not sought to fight for their prerogatives in this area and they would only fight about something on which they felt strongly, given their heavy dependence on public funding. The teacher trainers have gone along with the new policies *faute de mieux* and a lot less is heard now about their left-wing ideological baggage. It is also true that there are other reasons for the poor performance of England's cricketers and footballers which no longer has to be blamed on anti-competitive school teachers.

Whatever the attitudes attributed to the teaching profession and the teacher educators and trainers, there seems to be a common acceptance that the quality of new entrants is high. There is still 'wastage' and not long ago a newly appointed opposition spokesman rediscovered the PIT—the Pool of Inactive Teachers of yesteryear. There is probably still a widespread distrust of educational theorists of both the saloon bar kind and the academics in university departments. The keen desire to blame the academics probably grossly overemphasises their influence on what happens in schools. Many—most?—students manage to forget the lectures they sit through once the examinations are over. The critics flatter the academics at the same time as berating them. This only serves to reinforce the case for internship schemes and similar attempts to mobilise professional resources from among the teaching profession for the training of new teachers and for making a reality of a Jamesean third cycle.

References

Hoyle, E. & John, P. (1998) Teacher Education: the prime suspect, *Oxford Review of Education*, 24(1), 69-82.

INDEX